InterPersonal Skills
Skills that Matter in Getting Along with People!

Gerard Assey

InterPersonal Skills

By
Gerard Assey
© Copyright 2022 by Author

Published by:
Gerard Assey
19/18, Palli Arasan Street
Anna Nagar East
Chennai - 600 102

ISBN: 978-93-92492-38-9

Table of Contents

- ✓ Preface
- ✓ Importance of Developing Great Interpersonal Skills
- ✓ What is a Good Relationship? Defining a Good Relationship
- ✓ Types of Work Relationships
- ✓ Where and with Whom to Build Good Relationships
- ✓ Factors Affecting and Influencing Relationships
- ✓ 5 Unhealthy Patterns of a Team
- ✓ The 4 Key Components of Healthy Relationships
- ✓ Attributes that will help your Interpersonal Skills
- ✓ Why Self-Esteem Matters too: How to Build a High Self-Esteem!
- ✓ Managing You: Positive First Impressions!
- ✓ Watch your Body Language: People go by what they see!
- ✓ Meeting and Greeting
- ✓ Asking the Right Questions and Listening are the KEYS!
- ✓ Trust, Respect and Understanding-The 3 Key Pillars
- ✓ Giving and Receiving Feedback
- ✓ Handling External Working Relationships
- ✓ Managing Difficult and Challenging Relationships
- ✓ Addressing Differences and Diversity
- ✓ Dealing with Criticism

- ✓ Keeping Discussions from Turning into Arguments
- ✓ Resolving and Managing Conflicts
- ✓ How to Win People's Cooperation
- ✓ Final Keys for Building Strong Relationships
- ✓ Having the Right Conversations
- ✓ Effective Networking Skills
- ✓ Tips to Negotiate Effectively
- ✓ Your Interpersonal Skills when Overseas
- ✓ Conclusion
- ✓ About the Author

Preface

Interpersonal skills are essential in building positive workplace relationships and vital for your career and organizational success. These are the skills we use every day when we communicate and interact with other people, both individually and in groups and include a wide range of skill sets- most importantly being communication skills such as listening, effective speaking, and the ability to control and manage your emotions.

Relationships can affect the satisfaction on the job, as well as one's ability to advance and gain recognition for the achievements. We all work with others in our daily working life to produce the products and services that we provide to our customers. It is therefore important to maintain happy relationships with all those people we work with to ensure that our work gets done efficiently, and they receive the right type of service required. And for this, healthy relationships require a level of interpersonal interaction, trust, and rapport that is also required to sustain relationships in our personal lives. From that standpoint, we use the same competencies and skill sets for building healthy relationships in all facets of our lives.

It is no exaggeration to say that interpersonal skills are the foundation for success in life. People with strong interpersonal skills tend to be able to work well with other people, including in teams or groups, formally and informally. They communicate effectively with others, whether family, friends, colleagues, customers or clients, maintaining better relationships at home and at work. Therefore building effective workplace relationships is an extremely important skill for every employee. The strength of our relationship building skills can also affect our ability to negotiate effectively, deliver products and projects, meet deadlines and make progress in our career.

This powerful guide will therefore help provide the necessary components of healthy relationships as a way to understanding and leveraging on the relationships you have in your organization.

You will be able to:

- ✓ Build and maintain healthy relationships in your work environment.
- ✓ Apply the techniques and skills that promote good and healthy team relations.
- ✓ Effectively get work done through others.
- ✓ Tremendously help you in being a better listener and effectively ask the right questions to steer healthy and productive conversations.
- ✓ Effectively handle conflict and treat each other with mutual respect and goodwill.
- ✓ Increase productivity and work satisfaction.
- ✓ Achieve moral support and assistance with meeting difficult timelines.
- ✓ Develop and manage peer-to-peer relationships and your "social network."
- ✓ Communicate more effectively with staff, superiors, customers and vendors, helping you negotiate effectively.
- ✓ Overall, help Improve in your personal growth

Various strategies are provided as tools for working with and through others. When you build positive relationships, you feel more comfortable with your interactions and less intimidated by others. You feel a closer bond with the people you spend the majority of your time working with. For a lot of people, relationship building isn't natural or easy to do. Most refuse to admit this is a concern, because it is a basic common-sense concept, and they assume they already know how to do it. However, everyone, even the most outgoing engaging personalities, can improve their skills in this critical area. Your ability to create and maintain healthy and productive relationships through interpersonal skills with people at all levels of the organization is an important factor in your ultimate effectiveness as a leader

So go ahead and build on this important skill!

Importance of Developing Great Interpersonal Skills

Ethologists and Zoologists can tell us of what exactly happens in the animal kingdom. When observing the natural behavior in the animal kingdom, there are clear signs of rules of behavior between one another. The young monkey does not mess around with the other bigger animals and when lions are feeding on a freshly killed carcass the hyenas know very well that they better keep a good distance. And, nobody has taught them any of this. All of this behavior seems to be instinctual or intuitive but it gives a very clear purpose and message of maintaining order within a kingdom. So how much more with us, the human beings- considered with super intelligence! And yet, sadly, this is most times the very reason for chaos in organizations, families and even with some nations.

Human beings are naturally social creatures- we crave for friendship and positive interactions, just as we do for food and water. So it makes sense that the better our relationships are at home and work, the happier and more productive we're going to be.

It is interesting to see what came about from a recent study conducted on the top 500 CEO's worldwide. The survey asked each of these top 500 CEO's the following question: *"If you are to retire or to step down and if you had to look for a person to take your place, what are some of the traits that you would look for in the new CEO?"* Well, several different traits came about in that list, but I want to share just the top 3. Any guesses as to what they could be?

Right on top of the list as number 1, was 'Integrity'. And this should not come as a surprise, as if this ingredient is missing in the top man, you could imagine the state of the rest in the organization. What followed as number 2 was 'Communication and Presentation Skills', with 'Inter-personal Skills and Relationship Building' (the ability to get along with others, in a team, or as a team leader etc) ranking as number 3.

Most certainly, as can be seen again, this is one of the most essential skills, especially as you keep moving up the ladder. The higher you go up, the more crucial this skill becomes.

Good working relationships give us several benefits- to the individual as well as the organization:

- ✓ People help people they know, like and trust and when you help others, they will help you
- ✓ When co-workers help each other, the company moves forward
- ✓ Our work is more enjoyable when we have good relationships with those around us
- ✓ People are more likely to go along with changes that we want to implement
- ✓ We tend to be more innovative and creative with the cooperation of others
- ✓ Healthy relationships make us happier, motivated and more productive
- ✓ A strong network can help with career advancement
- ✓ Good relationships give us freedom: instead of spending time and energy overcoming the problems associated with negative relationships, we can, instead, focus on opportunities.
- ✓ Good relationships are very much necessary if we are to develop our careers. After all, if your boss doesn't trust you, it's unlikely that he or

she will consider you when a new position opens up.
- ✓ Will help to handle conflict effectively and treat each other with mutual respect and goodwill, thus improving morale in the workplace.
- ✓ We all want to work with people we're on good terms with as it gives us the peace of mind and a good night's sleep.
- ✓ We also need good working relationships with others in our professional circle- Customers, suppliers and key stakeholders are all essential to our success. So, it's important to build and maintain good relations with these people
- ✓ Helps with improved personal growth and development, as we don't need to spend much time handling interpersonal office challenges and politics- can focus on professional development.
- ✓ Increased satisfaction with our careers
- ✓ Increased comfort with presentations and team meetings
- ✓ Moral support and assistance with meeting difficult timelines
- ✓ Lesser attrition for the organization
- ✓ Having good working relationships with senior staff also means that we can benefit from their knowledge and learn from mentors.

What is a Good Relationship?
Defining a Good Relationship

Working relationships are the connections we form with coworkers, colleagues and managers in the workplace. Although the relationships we build with colleagues and managers may not be as intimate as those we have with family and friends, they are nonetheless crucial. Healthy relationships involve honesty, trust, respect and open communication between one another and they take effort, understanding and compromise from both sides.

There are several characteristics that make up good, healthy working relationships:

- ✓ Trust- This is the foundation of every good relationship. When you trust your team and colleagues, a powerful bond is formed that helps you to work and communicate more effectively. If you trust the people you work with, you can be open and honest in your thoughts and actions, and you don't have to waste time and energy trying to see what is happening behind your back- who is trying to stab you from behind.

- ✓ Mutual Respect- When you respect the people who you work with, you value their inputs, suggestions and ideas, and they value yours. By working together, you can develop solutions based on these collective insights, wisdom and creativity.

- ✓ Self-awareness- By taking responsibility for your words and actions, and not letting your own negative emotions impact the people around you.

- ✓ Welcoming Diversity- People with good relationships not only accept diverse people and opinions, but they welcome them. They are able to blend well instantly.
- ✓ Open Communication- We communicate all day, whether we're sending emails, on phone or meeting face to face. The better and more effectively we communicate with those around us, the richer our relationships will be. All good relationships depend on open, transparent and honest communication

Types of Work Relationships

The Workplace is where we spend roughly one third of our lives and, in the process, where we encounter a variety of people. Although dealing with workplace relationships of all kinds can be difficult, it can also bring a sense of togetherness and genuine friendship and therefore workplace relationship skills and ethics are imperative to having successful business partnerships with the people you encounter during an entire week- but those very same relationships can be tricky to navigate. Learning how to navigate workplace relationships can help to build your network and boost your reputation as a professional
Here are some of the type of Relationships you would need to work with:
Office friends: A work friend is someone you interact with in a more casual, social way. More than likely, these are people you collaborate with regularly or who share your workspace or work within physical proximity of you. Your work friends are often coworkers or team members you interact with at the office. These interactions may also extend to professional events or casual events outside of the office. You know enough about each others' lives to have some jokes, and they're a reliable shoulder to lean on. Your work friends serve as part of your support system, and maintaining these relationships is usually mutually beneficial.
Colleagues: This is purely professional. A colleague is the person on your team that you say hello to but don't go past basic chit chat or work-related conversations. They could be from other departments and usually on the same level and pay

scale as you and they're ultimately the people you actually need to work well with in order to accomplish your tasks. These people work closely with you, usually on a specific project. Together, you plan, develop and execute work that makes a big difference in your company. These relationships usually remain professional.

Manager/ Boss: This relationship is entirely professional and circumstantial. In most cases, there is little daily interaction, except for the professional meetings or briefings with your direct report beyond morning greetings as you'd typically be working more frequently alongside your fellow colleagues in similar roles. The manager assigns you the work and leads the team. This is a vital relationship, helping you grow in the company. They determine whether you receive a pay rise, promotion and restructure things like your hours or tasks.

Mentor/ Mentee: Typically, a mentor is sought out by a new hire or even a longtime employee looking to move up the ladder and leverage their talents with a little guidance from a seasoned professional. As a mentor, your advice and feedback should be timely, accurate and based on personal or professional experience. The mentor strikes the balance between professional and personal relationship. It's a more intimate version of a leader or manager, guiding you through the work landscape to help you succeed. While it's usually a one-on-one, the basis of your relationship is work.

Mentee – seeks guidance and advice from experienced professionals who have traveled your path. A mentee is an official or unofficial professional learner. If you support a mentee, your role is advisory and interactive. Your mentee is likely to come to you with questions about gaining skills, developing professional relationships and subject area expertise. Mentor-to-mentee relationships should be professional, sympathetic and communicative.

Client/ Supplier: A client/ supplier relationship is one between you and a client or vendor of the business or organization. Most for-profit companies maintain relationships with the customers they provide goods or services for. Depending on your role, you may interact with Individual customers, vendors, suppliers or people who represent departments within a client company.

Subordinates: If you hold a leadership position, you are likely to maintain relationships with people who report to you. Whether you are a team leader, supervisor, c-suite member or manager, the parameters of this relationship should be friendly, impartial, goal-oriented and communicative. Clear boundaries should be set to distinguish this supervisory relationship from other types of colleague or coworker relationships.

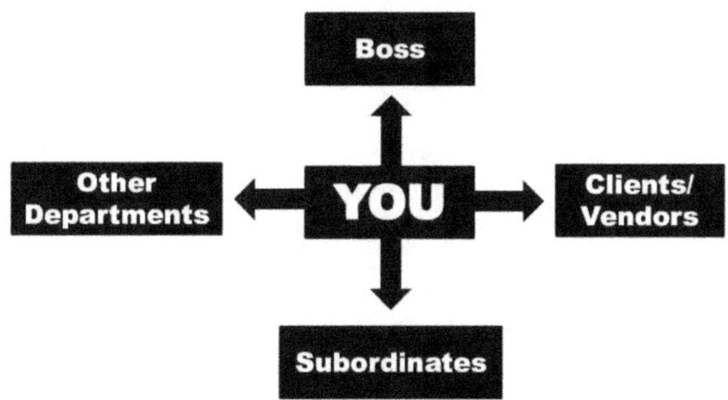

As can be seen from above, there are various types of relationships one will need to adjust with and move along if one has to be successful. However, most times, it would be these four types that will surround you- like a sandwich as in the illustration provided.

Where and with Whom to Build Good Relationships

Although we should try to build and maintain good working relationships with everyone, there are certain relationships that deserve extra attention. Here are some thoughts that can help you make a start:

A Mentor: A mentor is someone experienced, who has gone through the mill already and will help you navigate through life with you going through the 'school of hard knocks'. When a more experienced person teaches someone new, the knowledge transfer that takes place is unparalleled. Some of the most successful people have had mentors that have helped catapult their careers upwards on a fast track.

Key Stake Holders/ Sponsors: You'll likely benefit from developing good relationships with key stakeholders in your organization. These are the people who have a stake in your success or failure. Forming a bond with these people will help you to ensure that your projects and career stay on track. Once you've created a list of colleagues who have an interest in your projects and career, you can devote time to building and managing these relationships. You could begin by showing people in your organization that you're someone worth advocating for. This means you must be great at what you do and your work must be visible, by keeping your word and commitments

Clients/ Customers/ Suppliers: These are another group that deserve extra attention. Good relationships with your clients/ customers/suppliers can lead to extra sales, career advancement, and a more rewarding life

Competition: Your relationship with your competitor is equally important: When used correctly and in a healthy manner, it can serve as a motivation to hone and improve your skills and lead to improved performance, breakthrough ideas, and a greater drive to get things done.

Your Subordinates: If you are a leader that leads a team, then it goes without saying how important your team is for your success. Building and maintaining relationships within the team can help go a long way.

Factors Affecting and Influencing Relationships

What factors Affect and Influence Relationships?
We are all individuals and respond differently to various types of situations and other people.
We may find that we get along better with certain people in the organization than others and it may be due to many factors
So what are those factors that affect and influence one's relationships?
- ✓ Age
- ✓ Social background
- ✓ Same taste in music, sport, hobbies
- ✓ Same sense of humor
- ✓ Common job role
- ✓ Sometimes the same challenges or problems

Sometimes it can also be influenced by:
- ✓ Organizational structure (management and staff)
- ✓ Personality types (outgoing/quiet)
- ✓ Length of time you spend with people
- ✓ Outside influences that can color the mind

5 Unhealthy Patterns of a Team

Organizations fail to achieve teamwork because they unknowingly fall prey to 5 natural but dangerous pitfalls. Team members who are not genuinely open with one another make it impossible to build a Foundation for Trust

- ✓ Failure to build trust sets the tone for Fear of Conflict.
- ✓ A lack of healthy conflict creates Lack of Commitment.
- ✓ Because of lack of real commitment and buy-in, team members develop an Avoidance of Accountability
- ✓ Failure to hold one another accountable creates an environment of Inattention to Results

This occurs when individual needs (such as ego, career development, own needs, or recognition) are placed above the collective goals of the team.
On the other hand truly Cohesive Teams…

- ✓ Trust one another.
- ✓ Know one another's unique strengths and weaknesses.
- ✓ Openly engage in constructive ideological conflict. Engage in unfiltered conflict around ideas.
- ✓ Hold one another accountable for behaviors and actions.
- ✓ Commit to group decisions and plans of action.
- ✓ Hold one another accountable for delivering against those plans.
- ✓ Focus on the achievement of collective results

The 4 Key Components of Healthy Relationships

There are 4 Key Components of Healthy Relationships- they are easily remembered as the 4C's:

Conditions: Creating a supportive environment in which the relationship can thrive (awareness, authenticity, respect, forgiveness, understanding and trust).

Connection: Working together in ways that improve each person and the ongoing relationship. The goal is for each person to contribute to the relationship and grow from the experience (engagement, empathy, mutuality, vitality and empowerment). For best results, colleagues and business partners need to feel connected, working towards a shared goal. This level of understanding encourages trust and openness, and nurtures acceptance and shared values. Connection takes time to develop, and not everyone realizes its importance. But you can build it through constant feedback, involving openness and appreciation.

Commitment: The same as with personal relationships, commitment means making a mindful and consistent decision to invest in a working relationship. In business, both sides need to work towards its growth. Some people don't need reminding about the need to do this, or how to go about it. But we can all do better.

Communication: Even if you've made a connection and you're committed to your plan, everyday business pressures can lead to communication problems. Talking openly to address and achieve what is important to the relationship and the individuals involved (candor, listening, inquiry and closure)

Let's look deeper into the 1st C- Creating & Sustaining CONDITIONS for Healthy Relationships
Healthy relationships don't just appear or survive on their own. Managers and supervisors must begin by creating and sustaining the conditions necessary for them to thrive. And there are five conditions that are listed below:
- ✓ Awareness – Both people are aware of how the relationship is doing, based on observations and experiences.
- ✓ Authenticity– If both people are being themselves, less time is spent pretending, and more time is spent attending to what is needed.
- ✓ Respect – Honor and value each person, and appreciate any differences.
- ✓ Flexibility – Create an environment in which there is room for people to make mistakes. No Blame/No Shame.
- ✓ Trust –Trust is the backbone

The 2nd C- The quality of the CONNECTION: How do they relate to each other?
The second component of healthy and productive relationships is the quality of the connection between the parties involved. How do the people relate to each other and what results from how they do so? Below are the key characteristics of healthy connection
- ✓ Engagement – Participation with integrity.

- ✓ Empathy – Stepping outside their views to see the world from another person's perspective.
- ✓ Mutuality – Being in balance with one another. Even in hierarchies it is important to recognize that learning and enrichment can occur in both directions.
- ✓ Vitality – A healthy relationship increases your energy and sense of being alive.
- ✓ Empowerment – Dedication to mutuality in the relationship. More is possible because of the relationship than without it.

How can we evaluate the quality of these Relationships?

If any one of these components is not present to a great degree, you need to consider how you will work to improve the relationship.

1) How engaged am I with the other person in this relationship?

2) How willing am I to stand in this person's shoes with empathy right now?

3) How much respect am I showing this person in this encounter?

4) How much am I in reciprocity and mutuality with this person?

5) How willing am I to increase their power as well as mine in this situation?

The 3rd C-Is the COMMITMENT of every member in the Team. Just like a footballer who lets his team down by not showing up for matches, people who lack commitment at work can have a negative impact on their team's morale and performance. For this, every member must be willing to put in the time and effort needed if they want to achieve the organization's strategic priorities, by making sure to always keep their eyes on the prize. This will drive commitment in their personal efforts and set the right tone for building cultures of excellence for the people and organizations.

Here are some things that can help:

- ✓ Team members feel Valued: When team members feel that their work is making a valuable contribution to the organization they will be more committed.
- ✓ Purpose: Great teams have complete buy-in with their goals and objectives. They may go through a storming stage and can become disagreeable, but more often than not, this leads to better understanding and compromising on the best way of getting something done.
- ✓ Alignment of Goals: Aligning team goals to company-wide goals is critical to demonstrate how each team's efforts contribute to the organization's success. Teams with goals that are not organizationally aligned often lose their sense of purpose over time. Likewise, when individuals' goals are aligned with their group's goals, team performance improves.
- ✓ Clarity around Roles and Responsibilities: Ideally, each ones roles and responsibilities should be around their respective strengths and interests.
- ✓ The Team is stretched: Team members are challenged enough and that they aren't bored. Those who are excited about projects they are working on at work, will be more committed to their team and to the company.
- ✓ Transparency and Openness: Leaders should ensure that their team's goals are visible and

have been communicated to relevant parts of the organization. There is enough transparency that exists between top and lower level with opportunity to participate and contribute in various activities.
- ✓ Give Praise where Praise is due: Praise leads to confidence and renewed energy, and can give team members the final push they need when faced with a difficult task.
- ✓ Give people permission to fail: it's ok to fail and encourage team members to speak up if they spot any potential issues.

The 4th C- How people COMMUNICATE with each other. People in healthy relationships are able to have powerful conversations about things that matter to them, even when doing so is difficult.
Below are the characteristics of good communication:
- ✓ Candor -Get the essential issues on the table and address them with honesty, clarity and respect. Say what you are thinking in ways that promote the conditions for a healthy relationship.
- ✓ Listening- Take the time to truly hear the other person and their message with depth and respect.
- ✓ Spaciousness- Make room for each person to express themselves
- ✓ Enquiring- The other side of listening: being curious and seeking truth. Ask the right type of questions. Help others pursue their own answers.

✓ Reconfirm- Make sure that both people are clear about what has been discussed and agreed to in a conversation

Communication is one of the main KEYS to Healthy Relationships.
Here are some other things that you can keep in mind to work on this area:
✓ Acknowledge/greet people with a smile
✓ Use polite gestures
✓ Maintain eye contact, as appropriate
✓ Maintain correct (upright, alert) posture
✓ Genuinely show interest in what others are saying
✓ Listen more, talk less
✓ Ask appropriate Questions-Open & Closed (More on this in a future chapter)

Attributes that will help your Interpersonal Skills

This chapter will be addressing a very important attribute in order for you to be effective in your interpersonal relationships- The effects of one's attitude! So before we get any further on this subject, as a caution, organizations must be careful to hire the right kinds of people to prevent any potential problems among existing employees. And here's why…

In any environment, whether at home or at work, the tendency to think positively and approach each and every task with a "can-do" attitude can be really infectious. So when it comes to collaborating on projects, or in a team, the positive attitude can spill over into the way employees cooperate with one another. On the other hand, employees with a poor attitude about work and the tasks they are required to complete will have a negative effect on those around them. Just as a positive attitude is infectious and spreads to others, so too will poor attitudes have a negative effect on employee relations, resulting in division in the workplace, making it difficult for employees to collaborate with one another, as the poor attitudes spill over into how they treat one another.

If you are a student, business person or are planning to get into business, or are working for a business, you will know that while every business requires C.A.S.H. to survive and succeed….Every Professional also needs something to succeed, which I believe is more valuable than the CASH that comes in.

This is 'K.A.S.H.' because only when you have this KASH in you, you will be more successful in bringing in the CASH for you and/or the organization you represent, by ensuring and protecting the credibility and image of the organization

So what is this KASH?

- ✓ **K**nowledge
- ✓ **A**ttitude
- ✓ **S**kills
- ✓ **H**abits

Knowledge is all about your Company, the Products or Services that you offer, the Market and Industry/domain that you operate in, together with knowing of who are the other players or your competition that are in this industry. It also involves knowing where you stand against them-your strengths and areas that your competition has an advantage over you, along with being thorough on the rates, polices and regulations in your industry and market.

How effectively are you able to transfer any knowledge you possess, to the customer/ others to enable them to deal or decide upon the next step or you as their service provider is a skill.

Now there are various types of skill sets that people possess-Some examples for skills are:

Interpersonal Skills
Problem Solving Skills
Selling Skills
Networking Skills
Time Management
Team Working
Presentation Skills
Effective Probing Skills
Ability to present thoughts/ product demos

Effective Communication Skills
People Handing Skills/ Inter-personal Skills
Content Writing Skills etc

Now having Knowledge and Skills alone is not enough. There are many People you probably know of that have a great bank of knowledge along with the necessary skills, but yet have been total failures. Reason being they had a lousy attitude or very poor habits that killed a potential sale or the potential in them; that ultimately affected theirs and their organizations credibility

What you are seeing on the pie chart is the mental make-up of a Professional. As you will see, 50% has to do with the Attitude, followed by 25% on People Skills. In other words, if you don't have the required knowledge or skills, as you can see, you may be able to still succeed with the right attitude and people skills, because those two account for 75%. Now don't get me wrong, I am not saying that you should not work on your knowledge and skills…Absolutely no!

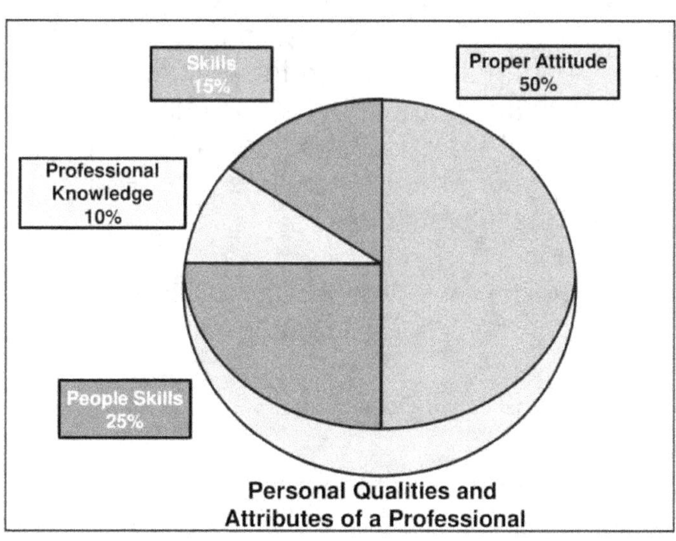

What I am saying is that given that you have the right attitude coupled with the right people skills, knowledge and skills, you don't have to guess where your career graph would be!

Let us look at this a little differently….Assuming you have the right attitude and people skills, which together comprise of 75% but lack the required knowledge and skills, well then, to me, with the right attitude you can easily learn them.   In any case Knowledge and Skills are teachable, but not Attitude! Attitude is the outlook or perception towards a given situation, and for any professional, this is extremely crucial and foundational! Attitude is made up from our upbringing, environment, exposure etc. It would therefore be very difficult or it would take a long time to undo a wrong attitude that has gone in all these years. And if you are working with people, like that of a sales or customer service professional, or in the hospitality field, then this is very important- as customers remember the wrong or negative attitude longer. You are the only thing the customer sometimes sees of your company- and this is the impression formed of your entire company- good or bad! It takes a long time to undo this negative feeling about your company in the mind of the customer.

Here are some of the Key Characteristics of Highly Professional people who are fabulous at their job:

- ✓ Highly Positive attitude
- ✓ Enthusiasm
- ✓ Communication skills (Ability to communicate clearly/to use positive language)
- ✓ Charisma
- ✓ Creativity and resourcefulness
- ✓ Patience
- ✓ Ability to ask effective questions

- ✓ Good listening skills
- ✓ Capacity and willingness to learn
- ✓ Alert and Attentiveness
- ✓ Multitasking
- ✓ Time Management and Prioritizing
- ✓ Stress Management
- ✓ Responsible
- ✓ Problem Solving Skills
- ✓ Systematic and Organized
- ✓ A Team Player
- ✓ Resilience-to handle criticism and negative feedback
- ✓ Adaptability/ Flexibility
- ✓ Empathy

At this stage it is important to realize that there are **3 A's of Business life**:
Ability, Ambition and **Attitude**
- ✓ Ability establishes 'what' someone does
- ✓ Ambition determines 'how much' he does
- ✓ But Attitude alone 'guarantees how' he does it!

Ability will bring one a pay cheque (check)
Ambition will get him a raise
Attitude alone will lead to success in everything!

Attitude is actually the 'YOU on the job. When ability and ambition in two people are about equal, how does the boss select one over the other for promotion? Here is where Attitude is the deciding factor. Attitude reflects a little plus- that something extra is given willingly though not required.
If you look at the word A-T-T-I-T-U-D-E itself, is it a mere coincidence that "I" comes first and "U" later? If this has any significance, then in trying to understand

the attitudes of people, we should first examine ourselves in relation to other people!

Because Attitude is so very important, this is why it is so crucial to fill our minds with the right positive thoughts because our thoughts work into decisions that form our actions and this continued action leads to a habit, which eventually makes up our attitude. Your habits today will become your attitude in the days to come. That's why it is important to check our habits as well. As an example: The habit of being late (at say your office), if not nipped in the early stages can lead it to becoming an attitude, with everything that you undertake being late or delayed!

Here are some examples of positive or right attitude:

Belief

Commitment

Desire

Ability to fail & learn from it

Persistent goals

Self-Motivation

Enthusiasm

Purpose

Self-discipline

Confidence

Creativity

Empathy

Go the extra mile

Self-improvement

Time organization

…and most of all the *PASSION!*

Great Professionals…

- ✓ Understand themselves and how their behavior affects others

- ✓ Have a positive attitude, which reflects in dedication to getting it right the first time, and commitment to helping others
- ✓ Know how to adapt their behavior to meet the differing needs of the situation
- ✓ A willingness to take responsibility
- ✓ Have the confidence to stay calm under pressure

Attitude Impacts Outcome

Steps to change your Attitude…

- ✓ Become aware of your negative attitude towards yourself, other people and situations and alter your thinking
- ✓ Think for yourself and become more constructive
- ✓ Keep an open mind

Remember: Changes are always: M.A.D.E…!!!

Developing GREAT Positive Attitudes is not something that happens to you-it is something you make happen…and like any change, it is not easy!

Here are some steps that can help:

M- Mental Pictures: Visualize who you are, what you want, how will you conduct and carry yourself

A- Affirmations: Add a new self-image by talking positively

D- Daily Successes: Build confidence everyday by looking at your positives rather than negatives

E- Environmental Influences: Surround yourself with positive influencers, read positive stuff, listen and watch positive information etc

You are what you think! To change any habits, you must first change any thoughts, feelings and values!

Changing Bad Habits into Good Ones!

Step 1: List your bad habits

Step 2: What were the original causes?
Step 3: What are the supporting causes?
Step 4: Determine a positive habit to replace the bad one.
Step 5: Think about the good habit, its benefits and results.
Step 6: Take action to develop this habit.
Step 7: Daily act upon this habit for reinforcement.
Step 8: Reward yourself by noting one of the benefits from your good habit

Demonstrating the RIGHT Attitude …
There are three simple things you can do to be successful in your life and in your business:
- ✓ Smile
- ✓ Show Interest in other people
- ✓ Be a Candle- bring light into the lives around you

How to stand out from the crowd?
- ✓ Put your SIGNATURE on everything you do!
- ✓ Do it from your heart!
- ✓ It's not what you do that matters, but how much love you put in what you do that matters!
- ✓ GIVE 100%

Remember: Success is in YOUR Hands

As can be seen, PERSONAL QUALITY is the basis of all other quality and is instrumental in determining your own future as well as your organization's profitability and future!

Why Self-Esteem Matters too: How to Build a High Self-Esteem!

Self-esteem refers to a person's beliefs about their own worth and value. It also has to do with the feelings people experience that follows from their sense of worthiness or unworthiness. Self-esteem is important because it heavily influences people's choices and decisions- especially when interacting with one another.

People with high self-esteem are also people who are motivated to take care of themselves and to persistently strive towards the fulfillment of personal goals and aspirations. People with lower self-esteem don't tend to regard themselves as worthy of happy outcomes or capable of achieving them and so tend to let important things slide and to be less persistent and resilient in terms of overcoming adversity.

So it is important to appreciate how low self-esteem can have a major impact on your daily interaction with others, if it is not at least basically understood and addressed.

An individual with high self-esteem is likely to build their network by having a positive, open and 'can do' attitude. Conversely, an individual with low self-esteem is likely to lack that belief in him/ herself to start with. They will convince themselves (and others) that they have little that would be of interest to others in any network.

Confidence versus Self-Esteem

A lot has been said and published with a great debate on the subject of 'Confidence'. A lot of people want to be more confident, without knowing the actual meaning of it.

A few points to note about confidence is that; it is 'External' and it is 'Temporary'. When I say external- I mean that in most times it is <u>not</u> in your Control- somebody else is most of the time controlling it. When I say it is temporary I believe that for a day our confidence levels fluctuate several times depending on situations, circumstances, the people and environment we are in. That is why we do not recommend that people aim at only Confidence.

Here is an example of what I mean:

You come into the office in the morning in a good mood-upbeat and all excited with a set of appointments you have for the day. However, your boss calls you into his cabin and pulls you up for a complaint that has come in from a top customer. What happens to your confidence level…One that was upbeat, is now down depending on how hard he came upon you!

Later, that same evening, you have bagged a huge order from another customer and that same boss now praises you as one of his best performers. What happens now? You are on top of the world, all up beat and charged up again.

As you can see in a single day your confidence levels can vary and fluctuate, which means they are temporary. Most times it is the effect or impact of others that have changed that feeling. It is like someone having a remote control on your life and your moods that can change or impact it every now and then.

A better, permanent solution to this is for you as a Professional is to work on having a High Self Esteem. First let us look at what is Self Esteem?

Simply put…It is how much you value or respect yourself! The more you value or respect yourself, then, when you do face such situations like the example we've just seen, you are able to stay above- your value if it is 100, stays 100 and does not change! You now know that your boss has pulled you up for something wrong that you had done- but that does not change your value- it still remains 100.

Building your Self Esteem

Say out loud:

"I am the Most Valuable Person at work".

"I am the Most Valuable Person at my work". (Repeat it)

It's true. You are the most valuable person. No one else can quite fill your shoes. No one else can be you. You bring your unique being to work every day. You bring with you your talents, your abilities, your knowledge, your skills, your personality, or just your plain know-how. You may not be using all of your abilities just yet. You may not be using them to the fullest. You may not even recognize how valuable a person you are.

Healthy Self Esteem, not narcissistic, self-indulgent, or arrogance means to appreciate the value of you as a unique human being with your own special talents and abilities.

The word "esteem" in Latin, means, *"to value highly"*

It would be impossible to value another person without first feeling valuable for yourself. When you place value on your own work and efforts, you can begin to find value in the work of others.

The Self-Image: Highway to Success

Have you ever said to yourself the following?

'I can't imagine myself being successful'

'I would like to, but I don't have enough experience or the right education'

'I can't get ahead because I'm too short, overweight, not good looking, my parents are poor, etc'.

The truth is most people talk themselves into failure and dejection. The result is the Fear of Trying.

Most of us know of or have read about common, everyday people who have become uncommonly productive and successful in their work and careers; individuals who have overcome enormous outer obstacles and inner roadblocks to become great.

Yet many people can't imagine doing such things themselves. They say, "*Yes, he could do it or she's doing it, but I can't because of__________*".

They develop the habit of failure. And it takes two forms:

Failure Reinforcement-the habit of looking back at past problems

Failure Forecasting-the habit of imagining the worst in the future

Because they lack sufficient self-esteem to believe in the validity of their dreams, they don't prepare for their achievement, and therefore are going down a dead-end street.

No wonder so many people feel trapped. Failure becomes set in their self-images.

Never put yourself down- the workplace is full of put-downs- Don't do it yourself!

Self Esteem Takes Practice

Believe in yourself, no matter how long it takes or how tough it may seem at times.

There was once a college professor whose wife had a hearing deficiency. In trying to invent a device to enhance her hearing, he created something more complex that he thought might be useful to the public. He traveled throughout the New England states trying to find venture capital to take his idea into production. But businessmen everywhere laughed at him. *"Ideas are a dime a dozen."* They said: *"The project is doomed to failure."* Thank goodness, Alexander Graham Bell had the self-esteem to hang in there even when his only reward was his belief in himself.

Often we put imaginary barriers in our paths when no such barriers actually exist. In the 1940s, the greatest physicist and aeronautical engineers believed that the sound barriers could not be broken- that everyone or anything would be shattered when it approached the speed of sound. One lone pilot, Chuck Yeager, didn't believe it. He didn't think there was such a thing as sound "barrier". And indeed, he flew right through it.

Your Formula for Building a High Self-Esteem

How much you like yourself is the core energy force that determines your personality.

All STAR Performers have a program or formula for building self-esteem.

Steps You Can Take To Feel Better:

1. Action precedes feeling. Act your way into feeling something. Action triggers emotion. The role of pretending- act happy!

2. Set clear goals, so you can feel like a winner. Establish a VICTORY LIST for all your accomplishments. Set income goals (the WHAT) and personal goals (the WHY)

3. Accept 100% responsibility. "IF IT'S TO BE, IT'S UP TO ME." Or "IF IT'S ALL FOR ME, IT'S UP TO ME". No excuses, no blaming.

4. Commit yourself to excellence. LEARN TO BE THE BEST in whatever you do. Say to yourself: *'I'M THE BEST (and) I LOVE MY WORK'*

5. Mental Rehearsal: Visualize the outcomes you desire, especially before you go to sleep at night. See yourself as strong, confident and relaxed, and see your customers responding positively.

6. Get yourself a small note pad. Every night write down at least 3 positive things you did for that day- (it could be as small as even helping a person cross the road). Forget the negatives. Most times we go to bed filling our minds with all the negatives that occurred during the day. Just reverse it now. Look at only the positives. At the end of the year, you would have over one thousand positive things about you. Do you need any else then to tell you?

7. Believe in yourself-FAITH! Believe in yourself, your company and your products.

8. INTEGRITY AND HONESTY. They are at the root of success in sales. Never expect to be successful without being willing to pay the price. Never expect the rewards without working. Don't look for shortcuts.

9. Have confident expectations. Look for the good in every situation. Expect the best.

10. Practice the Law of Increasing Returns-the more your give thanks, the more you will have thanks for

Managing You: Positive First Impressions!

Have you ever wondered about the impressions you could create even before you open our mouth?

In a study carried out that I am about to share with you now, you will notice that people place more emphasis on what they SEE rather than on what they HEAR. So this only tells us that we need to be very careful with our body language and what we are projecting.

According to studies carried out, Communication takes place in 3 forms:

- ✓ Your Words
- ✓ Your Tone and
- ✓ Your Body Language.

Where 55% has to do with your Body Language or what others 'See'

7 % has to do with 'What' you say or your words

Whilst 38% has to do with 'How' those words are said, which is your Tone or voice modulation

With people going by what they SEE first rather than what they HEAR, it makes it very important for us to therefore project the RIGHT image upfront. That's the first impression that has been formed-good or bad! If it is good, then very good for you, but if it is bad, then so sad! Because…now you have double work to undo the wrong impression that has already gone into the mind and to now fill it with the right impression.

They say 90% of lasting impressions are created in the first 90 seconds. That can be really dangerous, but surprisingly that is true! So we have to be very careful, with what are we projecting as soon as someone sees us, because that's what they will remember.

It is also a reason why we tend to remember a song seen on a television set better than when heard through a radio. The same logic applies at a job interview with your resume and the presentation of it! Then at the interview-the interviewer has made up his mind to a great extent as you walk in, even before you have opened your mouth. Your bio-profile or the interview process is only a confirmation of the decision already made in the mind of the interviewer.

Why is Tone next important after Body Language? Simply because you can say a same sentence with a different tone and that can change the entire meaning

Eg; "Mary come here" is a simple sentence. But depending on the right tone, this one sentence could turn out as an 'order 'or a 'request'.

Another stronger example: "Hang him not let him go"…could be death or life depending on how it is said. Example: 'Hang him, not let him go'! Or 'Hang him not, let him go'!

Now, if it is face to face, we may be able to save the situation, but when on the phone with the other person not able to see you, it could lead to miscommunication if the right tone is not used.

As seen earlier, with people going by what they 'See' first rather than what they 'Hear', it makes it so very important for us to therefore project the RIGHT image upfront. It basically involves Selling Yourself first!

Before a customer buys anything or decides to do business with you or the company that you represent, he needs to first be sold on you because you are what he sees about your company to him.

Your company could have a several floor building, with several offices all across the globe. But to the person doing business with you, what he sees in you is the impression he has formed of your company! Because…90% of lasting impressions are created in the first 90 seconds

A person forms an impression of you, usually in less than ten seconds, based on a combination of some of these attributes:

Posture, Walk
Body language
Attire, Clothing
Physical characteristics
Smile, Facial features
Handshake
Cleanliness, Grooming
Scent, perfume
Eye contact
Perceived Confidence

In a study, men and women were asked to list the attributes they found attractive and unattractive in someone they met. And here is the list of some of the top responses:

Qualities that create a Positive Impression:
- ✓ Warmth
- ✓ Sense of humor
- ✓ Imagination
- ✓ Fitness
- ✓ Individuality
- ✓ Positive body language
- ✓ Conversational ability
- ✓ Creativity
- ✓ Kindness

Qualities that create a Negative Impression
- ✓ Self-centered
- ✓ Closed minded
- ✓ Judgmental
- ✓ Lack of manners
- ✓ Poor conversational ability
- ✓ Negative attitude
- ✓ Indecisiveness
- ✓ Lack of integrity
- ✓ Complaining and whining
- ✓ Politics and Power games
- ✓ Manipulation

Making a Great First Impression

If you want to make a good impression, know that you need to project **3 C's:**

- ✓ Confidence
- • Have a straight but relaxed posture. Hold your head high and steady. Don't slouch or slump.
- • Move in a natural, unaffected manner.
- • Maintain eye contact with the people you are talking to.
- ✓ Competence
- • Exhibit your knowledge when required. Know your way around the agenda. Be prepared for the meeting. Bring supportive materials to emphasize your points.
- • Answer questions in a clear and professional manner, avoiding the use of slang or technical jargon.
- • Ask relevant questions if needed.
- ✓ Credibility
- • Arrive on time.
- • Be presentable (well-groomed and mindful of dress codes)

- Keep true to your word.
- When uncertain, err on the side of what you presume is conservatism. And be observant; check if people are becoming uncomfortable.
- Etiquette mishaps can range from merely embarrassing to potentially insulting to the other person. When you realize that you have committed a faux pas, apologize immediately and ask how you can make up for it

Appearance IS Everything! It starts with your Personal Grooming

Paying attention to your grooming by taking care of your cleanliness and your clothing demonstrates respect for yourself and for others- the key words being neat and clean.

- ✓ A general rule of thumb is: the more expensive the products/services you sell, the more professional you should look-Customers make assumptions about you based on your appearance.
- ✓ If it's an expensive product you are selling, the customer is bound to think: "How can this person help us make this expensive purchase when he can't even afford a proper wardrobe and take care of himself?"

Projecting the Right Image!

- ✓ How you dress, how you groom yourself and how you handle yourself in public is all part of your "packaging"
- ✓ Like product packaging, you can present yourself to be most appealing. And, you can present yourself differently according to the time and place.
- ✓ Presence is how you "present" yourself- it's your self-confidence, poise and appeal.

According to Drew Westen, in his fabulous book "The Political Brain" one of the main determinants of electoral success," he explains, "is simply a candidate's curb appeal". Curb appeal is the feeling voters get when they 'drive by' a candidate a few times on television and form an emotional impression! Personal Curb Appeal is primarily a nonverbal process.

How's your Personal Curb Appeal? When your co-workers, clients, and business partners "drive by" you, how do you come across? Here are a few tips to keep in mind:

- ✓ Dress for success: Always dress and see yourself for the next level!
- ✓ Your motto should be: "Wear great clothes. You never know whom you'll meet!" When it comes to curb appeal, the way you dress matters. Clothing has an effect on both the observer and the wearer.
- ✓ Dressing for success doesn't necessarily mean you have to wear a suit to work. Many organizations have a more casual dress code. But it does mean that whatever you wear should help you make the statement that you are a competent professional.

The finest clothing made is a person's skin, but, of course, society demands something more than this- Mark Twain

Watch your Body Language: People go by what they see!

As we've seen, people form 90% of their opinion of us in the first 90 seconds, a good example of just how powerful first impressions are! Being dressed for success is good but not enough in the competitive times in which we live. How many people do you know that impress us with their clothes but fail to impress us in other ways? Body language is the way you stand, sit, the way you move, and the way you present yourself. A major percentage of what we communicate has nothing to do with words.

We communicate in a lot of other ways-by the way we sit, stand, tense our facial muscles, tap our fingers, shuffle our feet and uncross or cross our legs. Without saying a word, our body language is broadcasting so many things about us!

So here are some quick tips on what to do and not do!

How to Look Interested

- ✓ Make strong eye contact
- ✓ Tilt your head slightly
- ✓ Don't fidget
- ✓ Look upward
- ✓ Lean forward slightly, weight on balls of feet.

 When someone is friendly, we also think of him as trustworthy, sincere and reliable.

How to Stand the Right Way

- ✓ Stand squarely in front of the person to whom you are speaking.
- ✓ It might sound strange, but you expose your heart and body.
- ✓ Don't turn sideways.

- ✓ Meet their eyes in a friendly but steady gaze.
- ✓ Smile in a warm, relaxed way
- ✓ Don't hold a book or purse in front of you or cross your arms.
- ✓ Use open hand gestures.

Maintaining the Right Physical Distance
- ✓ If you watch a crowd, you will notice that people stand at different distances from each other.
- ✓ Less than 18 inches: intimate
- ✓ 18 inches- 2.5 feet: close friends in a social gathering. You can hold out your arm and you can stick your thumb in the other person's ear! Try it!
- ✓ 2.5-4 feet: most people in a casual setting
- ✓ 4-12 feet: strangers
- ✓ 12 feet: a group of strangers
- ✓ If you get too close, the other person will grow tense or withdraw

Making Eye Contact
- ✓ The eyes have it. Well, they truly do, and can project confidence when there are no words.
- ✓ To be a good listener, let your eyes convey: "I'm listening"

Here are some Signs that can indicate Nervousness. Try to work on controlling these:
- ✓ Eyes darting back and forth
- ✓ Tensing of the body
- ✓ Contraction of the body
- ✓ Shifting one's weight from side to side
- ✓ Rocking in chair
- ✓ Crossing and uncrossing the arms or legs
- ✓ Tapping hands, fingers, or feet

- ✓ Adjusting or fiddling with pens, cups, eyeglasses, jewelry, clothing, fingernails, hair, or hands wringing hands
- ✓ Clearing the throat
- ✓ Coughing nervously
- ✓ Smiling nervously
- ✓ Biting the lip
- ✓ Looking down
- ✓ Chewing nails or picking cuticles
- ✓ Putting hands in pockets

And here are some Signs that can indicate Boredom. Try and work on controlling these too:

- ✓ Moving your body frequently
- ✓ Letting your eyes wander
- ✓ Gazing into the distance
- ✓ Glancing often at your watch
- ✓ Yawning
- ✓ Tapping fingers or feet
- ✓ Fidgeting
- ✓ Picking your fingers or nails
- ✓ Avoiding eye contact

Sitting, Standing and Walking the Right Way

The Right Way to Sit- for a Lady: If you are in someone's home or at a big social event, never sit, till you are given permission to do so. The hostess may have planned on a particular place she would like you to sit. If no one offers you, then only take the seat of your choice. Walk towards the chair with good posture. Turn and feel the chair with the back of your knees, just to make sure that no one has "accidentally" moved the chair away. Sit down, keeping your back straight and your head up, while keeping your knees together and you hands in your lap. Cross your legs at the ankle or hold your feet together. In any event, make sure your knees are together

The Right Way to Sit- for a Gentleman: Walk to the chair with good posture, and as you approach the chair, unbutton your jacket. Sit tall with your back against the chair and knees slightly apart and both feet on the floor, with your hands resting just above your knees. When you stand up, remember to re-button your jacket

Standing: When you get up, keep your feet parallel but your knees relaxed. Ensure that your spine is long and straight, with your shoulders back, stomach in, chest high, chin turned up slightly and your arms and hands relaxed.

Walking: Stand as mentioned above and step with feet slightly ahead of your body. This promotes good posture

Other Points: Never lean on anything, as it denotes a careless attitude with 99% of your "presence" being lost when you lean.

Never greet someone with a handshake across the table (the only exception of course is when you're meeting someone and both of you are seated).

Always stand up when you are shaking hands. Greeting someone from behind a desk creates an instant barrier. Instead, always greet someone as your equal

Meeting and Greeting

Greeting someone you know is a vital part of courtesy and goodwill. All societies and cultures have some form of greeting that is basic to civilized interaction. The first point about greetings is to do them. It's important to say "hello" even when you feel a bit off or shy. It's also important to make introductions even when you're not certain of precisely how it should be done in that situation. Every greeting and introduction is an opportunity to demonstrate respect for others and to create a favorable impression of you to others.

Your goal therefore within the first few minutes of meeting and greeting other people is to make them feel comfortable and to put them at ease so they will want to do business with you. Doing so will make the first encounter and subsequent ones go smoothly and easily. Getting off on the wrong foot can cause a difficult recovery

So let's first start with the most important thing you could do when meeting someone that doesn't cost you anything, before we get into the etiquette of handshaking and business cards and the other areas: And that's your Smile!

Your Smile will take you a Mile! It's been said many times- smile when someone enters your office and do it with feeling. Nothing makes a client feel more welcomed than a warm and friendly smile. Check yourself in a mirror to see yourself as the customer might see you…SMILE!

A smile is an invitation, a sign of welcome. It says, "I'm friendly and approachable."

The human brain prefers happy faces, recognizing them more quickly than those with negative expressions. In fact, a smile is such an important signal to social interaction, that it can be recognized from 300 feet- more than a football field away.

Most importantly, smiling directly influences how other people respond to you. When you smile at someone, they almost always smile in return. And, because facial expressions trigger corresponding feelings, the smile you get back changes people's emotional state in a positive way. This one simple act will instantly and powerfully increase your curb appeal.

On the phone-Your customer will not hear it, but will see and feel it! It's such an important aspect that can say a lot about you! Remember, it's the first impression that will often be the one that they take away with them.

Handshakes and Business Card Etiquette
Handshakes

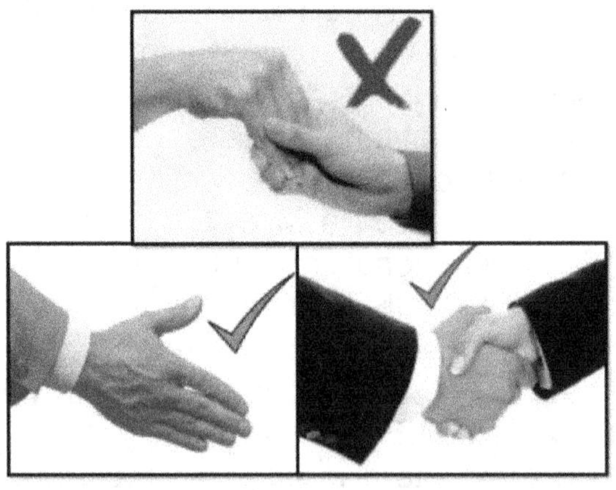

While it is good to give the other person a firm handshake, it is also important to note that 'firm' should not mean 'bone-crushing' but just comfortable enough for the other person. In other words your handshake should convey 'CARE'!
(Think of: **CAIR- C**onfidence, **A**ssurance, **I**nterest, **R**espect)
That is why we recommend that you practice the exact firmness of your handshake first with your own hand. This could be done by taking your left hand out: 4 fingers together and thumb up with the hand facing inwards towards you, as if it is a customers' hand. Now take your right hand the usual way you would use to shake someone's hand and assuming that your left hand is your customers' hand, shake as follows: Web into web first followed by the 4 fingers of your right hand around your left hand, with the thumb finally locking. Basically 3 locks…web into web, 4 fingers around and thumbs interlocked. Since it is your own hand, you will know what amount of firmness to use.
Keep practicing till you are comfortable with the right amount of firmness to clasp the other person's hand without it being 'bone-crushing' or the opposite- too limp (a dead fish hand shake!)
You can do this exercise whenever you are free, till you get accustomed to the exact amount of pressure to be used.
Now for some key points to remember while shaking hands:
A handshake can be initiated by either person and is appropriate when meeting a business associate in a social setting. Always stand when shaking someone's hand, and step out from behind a desk or table, while maintaining good eye contact and

posture. A handshake should end by the time you have finished greeting the person. When meeting an elderly or disabled person, allow them to initiate the handshake.

Business Card Etiquette

When presenting business cards, they must always be presented face up with the front portion of the card facing towards the customer/guest, and if presenting with one hand as in most western countries then it must be held by the tip not covering any part of the text on the card.

Most Asian countries present cards with both hands. Whatever be the culture, please ensure the cards are never kept in a wallet as they would tend to get folded or bent at the edges or corner. All cards must be in pristine condition, crisp with no folds, wrinkles or soggy edges. Whenever presenting the card, make eye contact, with a pleasant smile.

Remembering Names

One of the most embarrassing moments when introducing people, would be when you mess up on their names. Remembering names may be difficult for some people, but it's not impossible. It's a skill: something that you can improve with constant practice and application.

Here are some ways to remember names:

- ✓ Repeat: When someone is introduced to you, repeat their name. "It's a pleasure to meet you, John." This can help reinforce your memory of the name. You may also introduce them to someone else so that you can create an opportunity to use their name.
- ✓ Use mental imagery: We think in pictures, therefore associating an image with a name can help in assisting recall. Imagine a

person's name written on their forehead. Pick an imagery that works for you. The more striking or exaggerated your mental picture, the bigger are the chances of recall.

- ✓ Put it on paper: Write the name down as soon as you can. Write their details on the business card they give you so that you would remember them the next time you see them around. (But make sure you don't let the person see you writing on their business card.)
- ✓ Be genuinely interested: Remembering names begin with attitude. If you are sincerely interested in a person, then they would make an impact on you. If you adapt the attitude that everyone is interesting, and are a potential ally in business, then remembering names would come as second nature.

Positive Introductions: Protocol, Rank, Status, Titles and Forms of Address

The first rule for introductions is that they be made. Don't get too worried about making a mistake during the introduction. Forgoing an introduction altogether, however, is a mistake that may leave a negative impression. Remember, as seen earlier, First Impressions create lasting Impressions. With that said, we must realize that the goal for making introductions is to provide information about each other so that there is a common ground to carry on a conversation. Introducing people is one of the most important acts we experience doing in our daily lives, yet very few people know how to do it correctly. Knowing how to make a graceful introduction will not only allow you to make a good impression but it will also give you the confidence and power to nurture these relationships from the get-go.

Studies have found that most people would rather have you ask for their names than to stand in a group and not be introduced. Another equally embarrassing scenario that often takes place is when it's 'assumed' two persons know one another and the introduction may go something like, "You two know one another." It is for this reason, at many business and/or social functions name badges are provided. They are given for the simple reason to help your memory.

To start, here are some important business introduction etiquette rules to remember:

There are five "S"s to a great introduction:

1. Smile.
2. Stand up straight.
3. See: make eye contact
4. Shake hands.
5. Say: "Hi! My name is ...and I don't think we've met...

Arrival and Greetings when meeting someone
- ✓ As mentioned above, keep the 5S's in mind
- ✓ Repeat the other person's name in your greeting. Then say the name several times during the conversation
- ✓ Both men and women should be ready to initiate the handshake.
- ✓ Do not remove your jacket unless the host does. If you are uncomfortable, you may ask the host(s) permission to remove your jacket.
- ✓ It is considered acceptable for men to assist women with their chair but it does not always

happen; in upscale restaurants, wait staff may assist.
- ✓ Another rule of thumb is that you're not expected when leaving an event to tour the entire room like a politician. It's always proper to say goodbye to those nearest to you and always seek out the host of the evening

When being Introduced

- ✓ When introducing yourself or when being introduced always stand and extend your right hand.
- ✓ If the person you're meeting is much older or a higher- level executive, say, *"I'm happy to meet you, Mr./ Ms. Name,'* or *"How do you do, Mr./ Mrs. Name,"*
- ✓ You may usually call younger people by their first names.
- ✓ If someone says, "How do you do," in response to an introduction, the proper response is, "How do you do" or "Pleased to meet you" and not 'fine thank you' as " How do you do" is a greeting, <u>not</u> a question.
- ✓ Say "I'm pleased to meet you" in response to an introduction. If you are being introduced, stand unless you are physically unable to.
- ✓ "Hello Mr./ Ms. Jackson. It's so very nice to meet you". Continue to use proper names when addressing your host until they give you permission to call them by their first name.
- ✓ If, however, you were introduced earlier in the evening and had some conversation, upon departure it is OK to say, "I'm glad to have met you Tom" Or, If you're on the receiving end of

the farewell, reply "Thank you, Tom" or "I also enjoyed talking with you."

- ✓ If you are introducing more than one person, add a small amount of information about each person (any mutual interests you are aware of, how you know them, or their occupation). This gives them a starting point for a conversation.
- ✓ Always have business cards on hand.

What do you say when you meet someone? Introducing Yourself

If you introduce yourself to another person, provide them with both your last and first names. The other person may have an easier time remembering your name if you give them a small piece of information about yourself on what you do etc.

Always have your Elevator Speech ready! Here are some examples:

Good Afternoon, I am Gerard Assey and the Founder CEO of a Group: 'Citius, Altius, Fortius Unlimited, specialising in Corporate Training, one of the divisions being the only one in this part of the World to be listed under the 'Who's Who of Training' and ranked as No.1 on all search engines!

Good morning, my name is Philip Johnson. My company, PJ Display Products, offers convenient, lightweight trade show displays to make your booth setup easier"

Now take a few minutes and work on preparing your own unique introduction!

When Introducing Others

- ✓ When you introduce someone, start with *"Mr. A, I'd like you to please meet Mr. B from Company / Dept / Location,"* or *Mrs. B, I'd like to introduce my sister, and C. C, this is Mrs. B."*

✓ Never phrase an introduction as a command: *"Mr. A, shake hands with / meet Ms. B."*

✓ Next, say something about the person being introduced: *"Ms. B works in our Marketing Division;* or *"John is a former neighbor of ours at (Location)."*

✓ This little bit of information to the group about the newcomer provides a topic of discussion so that the conversation can flow smoothly.

✓ Refrain however, from long stories about how you met, or about the person's life or background.

✓ Avoid phrases of superiority like *"John works for me"*

Protocol in Business Etiquette

✓ Generally, a lower ranked person in business is introduced to the higher ranked person - not vice versa. (Executives, clients, important guests would fall into the "higher ranked person" category.)

✓ When introducing a younger person to an older person (Use younger person's first name, elder's Last - about 15 years is the deciding point.) The name to say first is the Older person's ("Ms. D, this is Jonny Alexander.") Typically, someone younger is introduced to someone older.

✓ When a client is visiting, everyone in the office is introduced to the client first.

✓ When introducing a Peer in your firm to an outsider, the name to say first is the outsider's. When a peer from another company is introduced to a peer from your company, the person from your company is introduced to the person from the other company first.

- ✓ When introducing a non official to an official, always say the Officials name first
- ✓ When introducing a junior executive to a senior executive, always say the Senior Executive's name first.
- ✓ When introducing a company executive to a customer or a client, always say the clients name first
- ✓ A family member is introduced first to your boss.
- ✓ At an event with a guest of honor, all other guests are introduced first to the guest of honor.
- ✓ Always present the senior citizen, guest of honor, or dignitary first. Be sure to use titles, not first names, when introducing a much older person, a doctor (physician, psychologist, veterinarian, Ph.D.), a member of the clergy, or someone of official rank.
- ✓ Use a dignitary's title even if that person is retired and no longer holds that position: "Governor Singh," "Mayor Abraham," "Colonel Johnson," "Ambassador Kapoor."
- ✓ An obvious breach of etiquette is calling someone by a name you prefer, not the name they prefer. An unflattering nickname has no place in business .If Charles prefers to be called "Charles," that's what you should call him and how you should introduce him - not as "Charlie" or "Chuck." If you don't call him by the right name, or if you mispronounce his

name, it's acceptable for Charles to correct you.
- ✓ If Charles prefers to be called "Chuckie boy," that's his business. Don't assume, however, that you know what people prefer.
- ✓ People are very sensitive about their names. Using incorrect names hurts your credibility and your chance of doing business with those you've misnamed.

Here are some examples that you can use to practice:

Situation 1 - Boss to Client
1. Introducer
2. Client: Mr. Samson
3. Your boss: Ms. Jackson

The introducer would say to the client, Mr. Samson, I'd like to introduce to you Ms. Jackson. Ms. Jackson is our Country Head. Mr. Samson is our client from Mauritius.

Situation 2 - Executive to a Client
1. Introducer
2. Office Manager: Susie Thomas
3. Client: Sanjay Kumar

The introducer would say to the client, Mr. Kumar, I'd like to introduce to you Susie Thomas. Ms. Thomas is our Sales Manager. Mr. Kumar is our client from Singapore

Situation 3- Junior Executive to Senior Executive
1. Introducer
2. Sr. Executive
3. Jr. Executive

The introducer would say to the Sr. Executive, Mr. Xxxx (Sr. Executive's name), I'd like to introduce to you Mr. Yyyy (Jr. Executive's name)

Overcoming Introduction Slip-ups
- ✓ Forgetting Names: Forgetting a person's name whom you have met before can happen to all of us and the worst thing you can do is to ignore them and not introduce them to your friends. The best thing to do is to apologize and say, "I am sorry, I know we have met but I can't remember your name." or say "I'm having a difficult time remembering your name." They should say their name and then you introduce everyone.
- ✓ Far ruder than forgetting a name, is not introducing people at all. People are usually very uncomfortable when they're not introduced as part of the group.
- ✓ When you're expecting several people and they are arriving separately, introduce each person as he or she arrives. Just politely interrupt the group's conversation and introduce the newcomer: "I'd like you all to meet Amanda Peters, the Communication Expert. Amanda, these are our associates from the southeastern office: Raj Sharma, Susan Abraham, and Mathew Thomas."
- ✓ If you're the one who's not introduced, take the initiative. Don't call attention and don't ask for an introduction. Just stand, extend your hand, smile and say, "Good Afternoon. I'm John Mathew, Mr. Fernando's Secretary and PA."

- ✓ If you are introduced but others are not, you may certainly take the initiative now, it's perfectly acceptable to start the conversation by introducing.
- ✓ There will be times when you do not remember everyone's name in the group- the best option in this case is to suggest that the people introduce themselves.
- ✓ If you are in a group and someone new walks up and no one introduces them, the polite thing to do is to stick out your hand and begin by saying your name. When this happens, it is a clue that the person you are with has forgotten the new person's name and can't introduce you.
- ✓ Not knowing one another: When you do not know if the people know one another, ask- "Have you met before?"
  If you are being introduced and the person doing the introductions hesitates, fill in the introduction details.

Saying Good bye

- ✓ When escorting your guests back to the main exit, thank them for coming, shake each person's hand firmly, and make good eye contact.
- ✓ Just remember that the main rule of good manners in greeting people and making introductions is consideration for everyone.
- ✓ Even if you don't know the precise etiquettes, if you put people at ease and show proper respect, your actions will be acceptable.

Asking the Right Questions and Listening are the KEYS!

Learning to ask better questions in our everyday conversations has enormous benefits on relationships. Firstly, asking appreciative questions improves one's emotional intelligence and demonstrates empathy to the receiver of your question. Also, asking well-considered questions expands the possibilities in the answer and has the potential to deepen a relationship.

However, sadly, we are biased towards telling instead of asking, because we live in a pragmatic, problem-solving culture in which knowing things and telling others what we know is valued .In order to build relationships based on dialogue and mutual respect, it is essential to learn to ask more questions. This shows care and concern.

Questions are a powerful tool to nurture relationships and make them effective and satisfactory for both sides.

If we start asking more questions we will immediately notice the benefits in our relationships with others:
- ✓ We'll understand the **people** we are relating to
- ✓ We'll focus on them and encourage **empathy**
- ✓ We'll allow them to express themselves and give us the **information** we want
- ✓ We'll stimulate their **attention** and their involvement
- ✓ It would indicate that we care and are genuinely concerned.

In order that the communicative exchange is effective and that the dialogue is fluid, it is important to ask the right question, and in order to ask our questions in an effective way, we should ask ourselves *"What do I want to obtain? What do I really need to know?"* this way the exchange of information can go straight to the point

So the art of asking the right questions requires the use of different types of questions. First let us have an understanding of the different types of questions that we could ask someone. Though there are several types of questions, for the purpose of this exercise let us look at just the 3 most important ones ie;

OPEN Questions

CLOSED Questions

FOLLOW-UP Questions

Depending on what type of answer you want from the other person, either of these questions are used.

Eg; If I asked you: *'Did you have your dinner'?*

Or *'Do you like this training session?'* or *'Are you going home this evening'?*

The only possible answer that you could give me would either be a *'yes'* or a *'no'*

That is why this type of question is called a 'closed question', because the only possible answer would be a one word- with either a *'yes'* or *'no'*

Closed questions usually begin with:

'Are you…'

'Will you…'

'Do you…'

'Would you…'

They are usually not very helpful in starting a conversation and extracting information. However, most people are more comfortable asking such questions.

The opposite of 'closed' is the obvious: 'open'. Open questions allow the other person to open up or do the talking and are used to encourage the other side to speak freely about a concern or expand on something already raised during the conversation.

Always remember this: Open questions generally begin with 5W's and 1 H ie;

Who?

What?

When?

Where?

Why?

How?

And they encourage the other person to open up and speak.

If we were to redo that example again using open questions, they would go something like this: *'What did you have for dinner?' 'How do you feel about this training?' 'What plans do you have for this evening'?*

These questions will certainly not fetch you a *'yes'* or *'no'* like how closed questions do. But they would allow the other person to open up with information which is what we could be looking forward to, by asking such questions.

Shooting out these questions without any logical order would also be inappropriate, as it could be unprofessional, could be irritating at times and most of all cause confusion in the mind of the other person. But if the other person was taken through a logical pattern, it could help lead him or open up to making the conversation two-way and interesting for both parties

Effective listening involves the use of follow-up questions and they are useful in several ways:

- They show we are interested and encourage the other person to keep talking.
- They increase the quality of the information gained.
- They help us to confirm our understanding of what has been said.

Before we can ask a follow-up question we need to listen to what the other side has said and wait for an appropriate pause in the conversation to ask the question.

Follow-up questions can also take the form of a question asked in response to a statement by the other side. They can reflect the information in the original question by beginning with phrases like:

So you are saying that...?

Does that mean...?

If I understand correctly are you saying that...?

Followed by a summary of what was said by the customer.

Let us see some examples now!

Examples of Open questions:

What exactly do you see the issue as Tim?

How can I help you solve this problem?

These Questions can help to dig into or search for details and are also called Probing Questions:

"Exactly how did this happen?"

"What steps did you take?"

Examples of Closed questions:

Did you receive the letter we sent you on Friday?

Are you happy with the service you have received?

Examples of Follow up questions:
What were you told when you rang us?
How quickly were you promised a reply?
In these examples the follow-up questions have been asked in response to the customer saying that he
1) Rang us previously,
2) Was told he would be given a reply

Listening Skills
Now while the other person talks, you would need to listen attentively.
'People were designed with two ears and one mouth, and that is the ratio in which to use them'!

How to be a Good Listener?
One of the greatest skills that one can develop is the skill of listening. The best professionals are the ones that do less talking and more of listening and that is why I believe God gave us two ears and one mouth- so we would do more listening than talking!

Listen Actively
- ✓ Focus on the speaker
- ✓ Keep an open mind
- ✓ Tolerate silence
- ✓ Ask open-ended questions
- ✓ Repeat the speaker's thoughts
- ✓ Listen for facts and key words

To be an "active" listener:
- ✓ Suspend judgment, initially
- ✓ Avoid distractions; when on the telephone don't carry on side conversations; when face-to-face make eye contact
- ✓ Assess what you heard

- ✓ Clarify and confirm
- ✓ Take notes of key points
- ✓ Never use your phone in the customer's premises! It's a big disturbance and bad manners!

Before you respond, assess the information you heard by asking yourself four questions:
- ✓ What has he/she told me?
- ✓ What can I do with this information?
- ✓ What else do I need to know?
- ✓ What questions do I still need to ask?

To show you're listening actively:
- ✓ Use terms like, 'Go on', Uh huh' and 'mmm'
- ✓ Stay tuned in/Watch for non-verbal cues

To show that you have, understood:
- ✓ Use, phrases like "I see," "I understand"
- ✓ Paraphrase, "So you want me to …"

Clarifying what they said:

In order to more fully understand what is being said we can make it clearer by asking for more detail:
- ✓ *You said that you were not satisfied with our service...Can you tell me why?*
- ✓ *You mentioned how helpful we had been. Can you elaborate specifically In what way?*
- ✓ *You said there had been problems in the past. What were they like?*

Clarifying and Reconfirming with Closed Questions

This is the time when closed questions are very useful. To clarify and reconfirm, restate in your own words what the other person has said and ask him/her to verify your understanding. An example would be: *'Mr Customer, Let me just take a minute to summarize, just to ensure that I've got the right information…You were mentioning that you were having a problem with….Am I right Mr. So & So?"*

After the other person has confirmed your understanding, you have earned the right to proceed with additional questions to gain more information about the situation.

Why summarize regularly?

- *It keeps complexities under control*
- *It tests progress*
- *It lets you restate what the other party has said*
- *It can help gain the initiative*
- *It can keep the discussion on track*
- *It can prevent misinterpretation, misunderstanding and subsequent bitterness*
- *In other words, summarizing helps you stay on top (but you take the point).*

By summarizing, you are making sure you have the right information and that you haven't left out anything.

Trust, Respect and Understanding- The 3 Key Pillars

Building Trust and the Measures of Trust

Robust communication is an essential part of trust in relationships.

Trust is the backbone for relationships. Without it, not much gets done well.

How to Build Trust?

The first job is to inspire trust. Trust is confidence born of 3 dimensions:

Character, Credibility and Competence

Character includes your integrity, motive, and intent with people.

Competence includes your capabilities, skills, abilities, results, and track record. Both dimensions are vital.

The foundation of trust is your own Credibility, and it can be a real differentiator. When a leader's credibility and reputation are high, it enables them to establish trust fast - speed goes up, cost goes down.

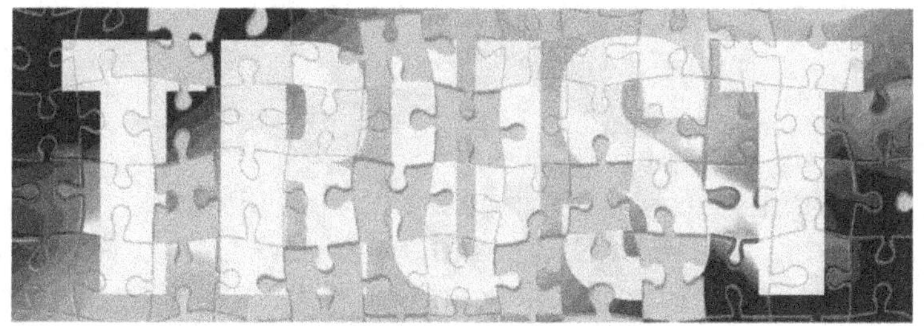

5 Common Measures of Trust

- ✓ Reliability: I trust that if I give this assignment to Rani, she will get it done on time.
- ✓ Candor: I trust that if I ask Raja for his feedback on my proposal before I submit it that he will be honest and constructive with me.
- ✓ Safety: I trust that if I share my struggles as a new manager with my peer she will respond with empathy and keep it confidential.
- ✓ Competency: I trust that if I ask Tom to present our group's report in my absence he will do a great job.
- ✓ Integrity: I trust that Rani will keep her word in the agreement we just made about her work.

How to Build Credibility and Trust

- ✓ Set a good example
- ✓ Keep commitments
- ✓ Tell the truth
- ✓ Be fair
- ✓ Don't have favorites
- ✓ Admit mistakes
- ✓ Be well-informed
- ✓ Understand the issues
- ✓ Share information
- ✓ Show respect

Building Respect

A mutual respect between individuals should underpin all working relationships. Demonstrating respect is fundamental to gaining trust and will form the foundations of a relationship in which ideas and opinions can be shared openly. Respect can be earned in a number of ways:

- ✓ Treat one another as equals. Even in relationships in which individuals have different levels of organizational seniority, colleagues should treat each other equally. 'Pulling rank' can make others in the relationship feel less valued.
- ✓ Share your knowledge with your colleagues. Offer them the benefit of your experience and encourage them to do the same.
- ✓ Recognize the achievements of others and make them aware that you value the contribution they make to your working relationship.
- ✓ Be honest. Committing to unrealistic time frames or making promises that can't be kept can be very damaging to working relationships. Be upfront with your colleague if you face constraints on time or resources, and suggest an alternative solution that is more achievable.

Understanding Others

Taking the time to understand your colleagues can be of real benefit to your working relationships. This means taking the time to learn what motivates and drives them to achieve their goals. Understanding can be developed in a number of ways, for example:

- ✓ Arranging an introductory meeting when you start working with someone for the first time to establish what you can expect from one another in the working relationship.
- ✓ Establishing shared objectives when embarking upon a new project or initiative to allow you to work towards a common goal.

- ✓ Using active listening skills during meetings and discussions. Active listening means listening intently to what someone is saying and making it clear to them throughout that you have heard and understood them.
- ✓ Finding out what each others' strengths are so you can agree on how best to share responsibilities when approaching tasks together.

Giving and Receiving Feedback

Feedback is likely to be more effective if:
- ✓ The person receiving it acknowledges the need for it; especially if the person requests for it
- ✓ It is timely; given near the time when the behavior has occurred
- ✓ It is skilful and professionally done
- ✓ If you consider the outcome to be developmental to both parties.
- ✓ You understand the motive behind it: Question your motive: If your motive is to show that you are better than the person or to put the person down, refrain from giving the feedback

What all can happen if you DO NOT provide suitable advice/ information or feedback on time?
- ✓ Misunderstanding
- ✓ Poor relationships/team working
- ✓ Wasted production
- ✓ Damage to machinery
- ✓ Unacceptable quality
- ✓ Waste of time and energies
- ✓ Customer complaints
- ✓ Drop in health, safety, security standards
- ✓ Credibility of organization affected
- ✓ Attrition (may lose even good people)

How to Skillfully Provide Feedback:
- ✓ Be descriptive, by providing information that describes the behavior and its impact on you; restrict the feedback to what you know e.g.,

behavior you have seen and how it has impacted you.
- ✓ It is about the giver of the feedback, not the person receiving the feedback. It is an exploration of the effect the person's behavior has had on you. (Note: the same behavior may not have that effect on others).
- ✓ Avoid exaggeration ("you always get this wrong"), labeling ("you are stupid"), and being judgmental
- ✓ Speak for yourself ("what I feel/experience when you ….") not for others ("Everyone gets upset when you ….")
- ✓ Don't press the person for any immediate response
- ✓ Face to face is the best-never by e-mail
- ✓ Observe the receiver's body language to assess the extent to which the feedback is being received.
- ✓ Adjust your feedback to ensure that the channels of communication remain open.

How to Skillfully Receive Feedback:

- ✓ Observe and listen actively to and when receiving feedback.
- ✓ Ask questions to clarify – "Could you give an example of that?", "When did that happen?", "Who else was there?
- ✓ If others where present during the behavior the feedback is about; ask them to offer feedback, what was the effect on them
- ✓ Acknowledge valid points
- ✓ Open yourself. Do not get defensive (you may feel it, don't act it).
- ✓ Stay focused on hearing what is being said.

- ✓ Take time to think about what has been said; if a response is necessary tell those offering the feedback that you will think about it and offer some response at a specified date/time.
- ✓ From feedback to negotiation of the relationship - "I would like …"
  What would you like the person to consider doing- "Because …"
  Why you believe it will help. "What do you think?"
  Invite and hear the response; explore options

When Giving Feedback, Keep the following in Mind:

1. Do it often: Virtually no one thinks they get enough feedback and that is because virtually no one gives enough.

2. Do not be shy: Give feedback as close to the event it refers to as possible. This way, what happened is fresh in everybody's mind and it will be easier to learn from it.

3. Give it some meaning: Always provide the context before you give feedback. For example "I wanted to talk to you about the report that you wrote yesterday."

4. Be specific: Talk about what went well and what could have gone better for the individual or the team.

5. Describe actual behaviors where possible: Avoid the "sandwich effect" (good-bad-good) - it comes across as untruthful and dilutes the impact of good feedback.

6. Give a wider context: Describe the impact it had and on whom. This gives an idea of how important it is.

7. Be generous with positive feedback: With positive feedback describe what it tells you about the individual. Find a few positives that you can provide.

8. Allow people a chance to respond: If they would like time to reflect, let them, and agree to talk about it again at a future date. Do not force people to talk about it though.

9. Remain objective: Do not let your personal prejudices get the better of you. Remember you are giving feedback for the other person's benefit and not to vent your own spleen.

10. Build an action plan: With critical feedback make sure there is an agreed way to progress. Find the right time and place.

Handling External Working Relationships

In many organizations, developing relationships with people who do not work in the same location as you (e.g. colleagues based elsewhere, clients and suppliers) is a key aspect of working life. In these situations, face-to-face contact is often limited, or simply not possible, so it can take a little longer to build relationships. Suggestions for successful relationships in this context are outlined below:

- ✓ Where possible, try to arrange at least one face-to-face meeting at the beginning of the relationship, to establish rapport.
- ✓ Without visual cues, it is easier to misunderstand someone when you are communicating by phone or email so ensure you maintain a straightforward communication style and avoid making comments, jokes or other uncalled for remarks that could be misinterpreted.
- ✓ Check understanding and any agreed actions at the end of phone calls. Make it clear in emails that you are available if further information is required.
- ✓ Maintain regular contact to keep the relationship on track. A short 'how are things?' email or a quick courtesy phone call can work wonders in helping to maintain a healthy working relationship.
- ✓ Always apply the same levels of professionalism as you would to internal relationships. Your conduct reflects your organization as well as you.

Managing Difficult and Challenging Relationships

Working in Toxic Places

Difficult people are part of every workplace you've ever known. Bad bosses can drive you crazy quickly and aggravating co-workers just add fuel to the fire. Most workers have found themselves saying "I really don't want to go to work tomorrow" at one point or another. But there's a fine line between wanting an extra day off and dreading going into work. Employees who dread work could be working in a toxic environment, which hurts productivity, employee wellbeing, customer relationships, and more.

Question to Ask when Dealing with Challenging Workplace Relationships

Here are a few questions to ask yourself (in no particular order) the next time you feel you are experiencing a difficult workplace relationship:

- ✓ Does it matter? Is this issue really worth your time and energy? If it isn't then don't get bogged down, just move on to your next priority. If it is, then it's worth the effort to resolve it properly.
- ✓ Why might it be happening? Everything has a cause. You may never know what that cause is, but if you assume that there is a good reason for the behavior then you stand a better chance of keeping your cool when you're feeling frustrated, annoyed, put-down, etc.
- ✓ Have you explained your position? Can you calmly and objectively tell them what they are

doing and the impact it is having on you? They may not have realized the consequences of their actions.

- ✓ Have you asked about theirs? They may not want to tell you but at least you are giving them the opportunity.
- ✓ Have you clearly defined the problem? Is it really their lateness or does your annoyance stem from other issues?
- ✓ Is there any common ground? If you talk it through you may find you both want the same thing. Anything in common is a good starting point to resolving the conflict.
- ✓ Can you both have what you want? If you assume that you can and then try to find a way to make it happen you're more likely to be successful (in other words, think positive!)
- ✓ If not, where is the acceptable compromise? What could you both give up and still feel fairly treated?

How to respond to difficult people: Use these strategies for success.

1. Watch your attitude. When dealing with difficult people, the most important thing to remember is to have ultimate control of your attitude. You always have a choice as to how to respond to a given individual. You can get upset and frustrated, or you can remain calm and handle that person with tact.

2. Stay calm, cool, and collected. Losing your temper and flaring up at the other person typically isn't the best way to get him/her to collaborate with you. Try counting to 10, taking a break, walking away from the situation, having a cup of coffee or water or even putting the person on the phone on hold for a short time. These techniques work because they break you

away from the situation, giving you time to think what to do. Someone who is calm is seen as being in control, focused and more respectable. When the person you are dealing with sees that you are calm despite whatever he/she is doing, you will start getting their attention.

3. Understand the person's intentions. No one is difficult for the sake of being difficult. Even when it may seem that the person is just out to get you, there is always some underlying reason that is motivating them to act this way. Rarely is this motivation apparent. Try to identify the person's trigger: What is making him/her act in this manner? What is stopping him/her from cooperating with you? How can you help to meet his/her needs and resolve the situation?

4. Let the person know where you are coming from. One thing that can work is to let the person know your intentions behind what you are doing. Sometimes, they are being resistant because they think that you are just being difficult with them. Letting them in on the reason behind your actions and the full background of what is happening will enable them to empathize with your situation. This lets them get on-board much easier.

5. Use your brain and not your heart, but have heart. In other words, do not use emotions to handle a difficult person. When you use emotion, you are just reacting. Instead, use your mind to deal with the negative person or situation. When you do this, you are in control.

6. Weigh the situation and consequences. Evaluate the situation and think about the consequences of your actions. See beyond the immediate. Anticipate what could happen and whether you can live with that. Then act in a positive, confident manner.

7. Attack the issue, not the person. It never does any good to attack people. Obviously something happened that caused the conflict. Get to the issue and focus on it rather than on the person.

8. Listen. Listen carefully in order to understand the other person's point of view. Block out your own thoughts, judgments, and priorities and listen to the other person's concerns and feelings. Be a dispassionate observer, by remaining detached, neutral, and above the emotion of the conflict. Observe, listen, and let the other person know he's been heard, but do not allow yourself to come down into the scene. You did not make the person difficult, and you cannot "fix" them. You can, however, limit their influence, and not reinforce difficult behavior.

9. Define the problem. Are you clear on the real issue of conflict or is it just your perception? Ongoing communication helps clarify each person's perception of the situation, ensuring that the problem is clearly defined.

10. Use facts only. Stick to the facts when confronting someone. You will get more positive results when you deal with the facts than with the emotions around them.

11. Focus on what can be worked upon or put to action. Whatever it is, acknowledge that the situation has already occurred. Rather than focus on what you cannot change, focus on the actionable steps you can take to forward yourself in the situation.

12. Maintain each other's self-esteem. It's harmful to belittle others, and this diminishes your professional image. When confronting colleagues, make sure you communicate in a way that allows them to save face. Treat the other person with respect. As the golden

rule says, "Do unto others as you would have them do unto you."

13. Re-instill the human touch by connecting with your colleagues on a personal level. Go out with them for lunches or dinners. Get to know them as people, and not colleagues. Learn more about their hobbies, their family, and their lives. Foster strong connections. These will go a long way in your work.

14. Focus on Future Behavior: People aren't the problem; it's the behavior that is the problem. A person can only change future behavior. A conversation filled with a history of mistakes generates defensiveness and shuts down communication.

15. Limit your interactions. If you have already tried everything above and the person is still not being receptive, the best way might be to just ignore. If you haven't been able to form any kind of useful relationship with your colleague then try to avoid working closely with them. After all, you have already done all that you can within your means. Get on your daily tasks and interface with the person only where needed.

Addressing Differences and Diversity

It is inevitable that, at some point, you will encounter challenges in your working relationships. When a difficult situation occurs, it is important that it is addressed promptly. There are number of ways you can do this, for example:

- ✓ Have an open conversation with the person concerned. This may seem awkward at first, but failing to address problems can lead to more serious issues. Outline your concerns concisely, supporting your points with examples. Stress your commitment to the relationship and your wish to find a solution that works for both of you.
- ✓ Listen carefully to your colleague's point of view and take their comments on board. Clarify any actions you or your colleague might need to take to help the relationship get back on track.
- ✓ Avoid the temptation to badmouth your colleague or approach the issue with their manager, before you have discussed it with them personally. If you are unsure whether speaking to your colleague directly is the right thing to do, take the advice of someone you trust in the organization, such as another manager or director.

What you could do to Manage Diversity
- ✓ Accept that differences exist and are healthy

- ✓ Discover, Understand, Accept and Inventory the differences that exist among your team members
- ✓ Affirm the value of Team members differences
- ✓ Make a habit to build others self-worth/ self-esteem
- ✓ Don't let Ego come between
- ✓ Make a habit to listen to others for better understanding
- ✓ Try looking at their views and perspectives with an open mind
- ✓ Keep asking: What are their positive traits that the team can benefit from

Dealing with Criticism

How to Deliver Criticism the Proper Way
- ✓ Choose the time and place carefully: Find a private place where you know you won't be interrupted that is convenient to both
- ✓ Listen impartially: Not showing any negative or defensive emotions when listening will stop you appearing vulnerable or fragile.
- ✓ Summarize what the other person has said: This means you have understood them correctly and also that you have taken it all in.
- ✓ Ask questions: The more specific the criticism the more helpful. Find out what you did and when that gave them their impression. This will mean you will not make the same mistake again.
- ✓ Be as specific as you can. Ideally, with examples. Do not generalize
- ✓ Avoid general and negative 'triggers.': Words and phrases that will put the employee on the defensive, such as "you always" and "you never."
- ✓ Criticism is rarely groundless but often exaggerated: Decide which elements are useful and what you can do differently to be more effective from now on.
- ✓ Focus on the future. Once you have covered the details, move on to the future immediately, on what changes you would like to see.
- ✓ Think about how the person who criticizes you looks at the world: Could they have been trying to help? Are they under pressure themselves? Think about why they have these

views about you. This could open up to some useful self awareness.
- ✓ Ask those who criticize you for their advice: By making them part of the solution, they are less likely to criticize you in the future.
- ✓ Thank people who criticize you: Not only have they given you free information but you have now also disarmed them.
- ✓ Reframe criticism which focuses on what went badly: Consider what positive steps you can take to improve in the future and what you have learnt from not succeeding.
- ✓ If you are angry, take it out on something, not someone: It is understandable to be annoyed but not very useful.
- ✓ Praise others for what they are doing well: It will give you the moral high ground and make you popular (as well as reinforcing productive behavior).

Keeping Discussions from Turning into Arguments

The only way you can make sure you never lose an argument, to paraphrase Dale Carnegie, is to avoid getting into one in the first place.

Tips to keep discussions from Turning into Arguments:
1. Do not argue: Refuse to get drawn into an argument. Respect the other person as much as you honor your own values. Be assertive without resorting to aggression.
2. Seek areas of agreement: Often we agree with people in principle but disagree with them in practice (we want the same thing but have different ideas of how to accomplish it). Find those areas of agreement. Make them clear. Try always to make the other person a fellow problem-solver, neither an opponent nor a friend.
3. Focus on interests, not positions: An issue is what we want or need. A position is a way of achieving it. Avoid getting attached to your positions so that you do not lose sight of your interests. It is often easier to negotiate and compromise around interests than around positions.
4. Try to see things from the other person's point-of-view: There is a reason why other people act and think the way they do - however illogical, wrong-headed, or misguided as it may seem to you. If you criticize them or show disapproval for their reasoning, they will only harden in their resolution. They will resent and resist you. Seek, instead, to discover their

hidden reasons, and you will find the key to their motivation.

5. Ask clarifying questions: Ask open-ended questions. As noted earlier under the chapter of 'Questioning and Listening', closed questions-like "Do you agree with my proposal?" –these limit people's ability to express themselves. Open-ended questions – like "How do you feel about my proposal?" will give them freedom and give you more information.

6. Listen: Spend more time listening than speaking (you cannot get yourself into trouble by listening, but you sure can start an argument by speaking). Listen with your body, your eyes and your mind as well as with your ears. Try to understand what people mean, without getting caught up in the exact words they say. Make them feel understood, and they will be much more likely to try to understand you.

7. If you are wrong, admit it: There is nothing wrong with changing your opinion, once you have gained new information or perspective. As a matter of fact, it is the sign of wisdom and maturity. Remember that you have been wrong in the past even when you thought you were right, and admit that you might be wrong this time.

8. If you are right, allow the other person to save face: You are trying to win people's cooperation, not to prove them wrong. Your kindness will do more to gain their goodwill than anything else. Do not let ego come in between

Resolving and Managing Conflicts

Conflict is a normal, and even healthy, part of relationships. After all, two people can't be expected to agree on everything at all times. Since relationship conflicts are inevitable, learning to deal with them in a healthy way is crucial. When conflict is mismanaged, it can harm the relationship and hamper progress. But when handled in a respectful and positive way, conflict provides an opportunity for growth, ultimately strengthening the bond between two people and can keep your personal and professional relationships strong and growing.

Successful conflict resolution depends on your a bility to:

- ✓ Keep the bigger picture in mind while focusing on the future.
- ✓ Manage stress while remaining alert and calm. By staying calm, you can accurately read and interpret verbal and nonverbal communication.
- ✓ Control your emotions and behavior. When you're in control of your emotions, you can communicate your needs without threatening, frightening, or punishing others.
- ✓ Pay attention to the feelings being expressed as well as the spoken words of others.
- ✓ Be aware of and respectful of differences. By avoiding disrespectful words and actions,

Healthy and unhealthy ways of managing and resolving conflicts

Conflict triggers strong emotions and can lead to hurt feelings, disappointment, and discomfort. When handled in an unhealthy manner, it can cause irreparable rifts, resentments, and breakups. But when conflict is resolved in a healthy way, it increases our understanding of one another, builds trust, and strengthens our relationship bonds.

Unhealthy responses to conflict are characterized by:

- ✓ An inability to recognize and respond to matters of great importance to the other person.
- ✓ Abusive, explosive, angry, hurtful, and resentful reactions
- ✓ The withdrawal of love, resulting in rejection, isolation, shaming, and fear of abandonment
- ✓ The expectation of bad outcomes
- ✓ The fear and avoidance of conflict

Healthy responses to conflict are characterized by:

- ✓ The capacity to recognize and respond to important matters
- ✓ A readiness to forgive and forget
- ✓ The ability to seek compromise and avoid punishing
- ✓ A belief that resolution can support the interests and needs of both parties

Steps in Resolving Conflicts

1. Acknowledge that conflict exists
2. Agree on a mutually acceptable time and place to discuss the conflict.
3. State the problem as you see it and list your concerns.
4. Identify the "real" conflict
5. Withhold judgments, accusations, and generalized statements ("always" or "never").

6. Let the other person have his/her say. Hear all points of view. Do not interrupt or contradict.

7. Do not allow name-calling, put-downs, threats, obscenities, yelling or intimidating behavior.

8. Listen and ask questions. Ask fact-based open questions (who? where? what? when? how?. See more on Question techniques under the respective chapter) to make sure you understand the situation. Ask exploratory questions (what if? what are you saying? is this the only solution to your problem? what if did such and such? are there other alternatives to this situation?). Avoid accusatory "why" questions (why are you like that?).

9. Reconfirm/ Paraphrase. Use your own words to restate what you think the other person means and wants. Acknowledge person's feelings and perceptions.

10. Stick to one conflict at a time- the issue at hand. Do not change the subject or allow it to be changed. ("I understand your concern but I'd like to finish what we're talking about at the moment before we discuss it.")

11. Focus on Present NOT past: Don't hold on to hurts- focus on what you can do to solve the problem

12. Seek common ground. What do you agree on? What are your shared concerns? Together explore ways to resolve the conflict

13. Brainstorm solutions to the conflict that allow everyone to win.

14. Request behavior changes only. Do not ask others to change their attitudes. Do not ask them to "feel" differently about something. Do not ask them to "be" different. If you want them to "stop doing" something, suggest an alternative solution.

15. Agree to the best way to resolve the conflict

16. Set a timetable for implementing it. Who will do what by when?

17. Gain agreement on, and responsibility for, a solution

18. Schedule a follow-up session to review the resolution

19. If the discussion breaks down, reschedule another time to meet. Consider bringing in a third party.

20. Work on building back your relationship

Guidelines to keep in mind when fire-fighting

Managing and Resolving Conflicts requires: Emotional Maturity, Self-control and Empathy. Here are some points to keep in mind:

- ✓ Make the Relationship your Priority: Don't look at 'winning' an argument- Be respectful of others view point
- ✓ Remain calm. Try not to overreact to difficult situations. By remaining calm it will be more likely that others will consider your viewpoint.
- ✓ Express feelings in words, not actions. Telling someone directly and honestly how you feel can be a very powerful form of communication. If you start to feel so angry or upset that you feel you may lose control, take "time out" and do something to help yourself feel better.
- ✓ Be specific about what is bothering you. Vague complaints are hard to work on.
- ✓ Pick your Battles: Consider-is this issue really worth the time/ energy. Eg; parking space- not wanting to surrender after circling 15 minutes...but if enough space around is it worth it arguing!

- ✓ Deal with only one issue at a time. Don't introduce other topics until each is fully discussed. This avoids the "kitchen sink" effect where people throw in all their complaints
  while not allowing anything to be resolved.
- ✓ No "hitting below the belt." Attacking areas of personal sensitivity creates an atmosphere of distrust, anger, and vulnerability.
- ✓ Avoid accusations. Accusations will cause others to defend themselves. Instead, talk about how someone's actions made you feel
- ✓ Don't generalize. Avoid words like "never" or "always." Such generalizations are usually inaccurate and will heighten tensions.
- ✓ Don't stockpile. Storing up lots of grievances and hurt feelings over time is counterproductive. It's almost impossible to deal with numerous old problems for which interpretations may differ. Try to deal with problems as they arise.
- ✓ Avoid clamming up. When one person becomes silent and stops responding to the other, frustration and anger can result. Positive results can only be attained with two-- way communication
- ✓ Be willing to Forgive
- ✓ Know when to let something go: If a conflict is getting nowhere, you can choose to disengage and move on!

How to Win People's Cooperation

1. Make people feel understood: Spend less time trying to make people understand what you want, and more time making them feel understood.
2. Find common ground: Show people how their needs, values and dreams mesh with yours. To do so, you have to understand their values and concerns. See things from their point of view. Be sympathetic with their feelings. Then show them how cooperating with you can help them achieve what they want.
3. Listen: Listening is the best way to make people feel understood and at the same time to find common ground. Ask open-ended questions, the kinds that invite people's careful consideration and honesty. Try to understand what people mean, without getting hung up on the literal meaning of their words. And acknowledge their thoughts and feelings (which is not the same thing as agreeing with them).
4. Do not argue: The person you defeat in an argument today may be the person whose cooperation you may need tomorrow. And the more you try to prove them wrong, the harder they will resist you. People may feel overwhelmed and stop arguing with you. But that does not mean you have won them over. Remember, most of the time, when you win an argument, you lose an ally.
5. Care about the people you want to influence: If you are concerned about the people you are trying to win over, if you value their needs and dreams, they will know it and they will reciprocate. They will communicate more freely, speaking their mind more

openly and listening more attentively. They will give you the benefit of the doubt and they will want to cooperate.

6. Be open for other's ideas: Do not try to impose your ideas or thoughts on others. Listen to and value the ideas of the people that work for you or with whom you work together. Be open-minded and feel confident with sharing the ideas with others. Even, request for new ideas to gain people's support and co-operation.

7. Help people believe the change is possible: People often know, although they will not often admit, that they need to change. They feel a vague uneasiness, sensing that things will not work out the way they want. But they persist in doing what they have always done, thinking they are doing the best they can. Show them a better way, but more importantly convince them that the change is possible. Do not just give them a solution but offer them confidence.

8. Time your request well: There is a time and season for everything, especially for asking for support. When people are feeling stressed out, anxious, angry, resentful or threatened, they are not really receptive. Do what you can to reassure them and to make them feel safe and you increase your chances of winning their support. Look for "moments of influence", times when they feel capable and confident, and make your best case then.

Final Keys for Building Strong Relationships

Finally, what can you do to build Healthy and Strong Work Relationships? Here are some thoughts that can help you?

- ✓ Work on developing your people skills: Good relationships start with good people skills. In other words, how well you collaborate, communicate, commit and deal with conflict.
- ✓ Identify relationship needs: Look at the relationship needs of others as well as yourself. Do you know what they need from you? And do you know what you need from others? Understanding these needs can be instrumental in building better relationships
- ✓ Establish a set of values or 'ground rules' for yourself and apply them to every working relationship you develop: Adopt a consistent approach and aim to achieve the same degree of trust, respect and understanding with every person you work with.

- ✓ Respect Others: Respect others and their opinions. Never make others feel neglected, and not being harsh on their face when you disagree with them. Respect their inputs and try to explain your point of view with a little more empathy.
- ✓ Speak positively about the people you work with especially to your boss: Always speak positively to others and provide quality feedback about the people you work with. Shared information- positive or negative often comes back to the person being discussed. That will build trust.
- ✓ Listen Actively: Practice active listening when you talk to your customers and colleagues. People respond to those who truly listen to what they have to say. Focus on listening more than you talk, and you'll quickly become known as someone who can be trusted.
- ✓ Set time aside to build relationships: Set a portion of your day towards relationship building, even if it's just a few minutes. Strengthen your relationships by aiming to get to know your colleagues better outside the workplace. Attend social events and group activities when you have the opportunity, to build rapport and spend time with your colleagues in a more relaxed setting. These little interactions help build the foundation of a good relationship, especially if they're face-to-face.
- ✓ Ask the people with whom you work most closely to provide you with some feedback on your working relationship and to highlight anything they might like you to do differently:

Agree on steps you can both take to improve the relationship, if necessary.

✓ Learn to appreciate others: Show your appreciation whenever someone helps you. Everyone wants to feel that their work is appreciated. So, genuinely compliment the people around you when they do something well. This will open the door to great work relationships.

✓ Write thank-you notes: Write notes of appreciation to the people who are doing exemplary work, making positive contributions, and going above the call of duty. Everyone likes to be appreciated and will feel closer to you

✓ Be Positive: Focus on being positive. Positivity is attractive and contagious, and it will help strengthen your relationships with your colleagues. No one wants to be around someone who's negative all the time.

✓ Be proactive and help wherever you can without being asked: Where possible, offer your knowledge and experience to colleagues and find a way to help with work your colleagues are undertaking. Ask how you can get involved. This will form a closer connection because you are working directly with others to help them meet their goals. They will appreciate your support and get to know you better, which is vital to creating a more connected working relationship.

✓ Manage your boundaries: Make sure that you set and manage boundaries properly – all of us want to have friends at work, but, occasionally, a friendship can start to impact our jobs, especially when a friend or colleague begins to monopolize our time. If this happens, it's important that you're assertive about your boundaries, and that you know how much time you can devote during the work day for social interactions.

✓ Always keep your commitment and deliver as promised: Nothing is worse than someone who fails to deliver on a promise or consistently misses deadlines. There is no quicker way to spoil your reputation and damage potential working relationships than failing to follow through on work

✓ Never gossip: Totally avoid gossip. Office politics and "gossip" are major relationship killers at work. If you're experiencing conflict with someone in your group, talk to them directly about the problem. Gossiping about the situation with other colleagues will only worsen the situation, and will cause mistrust and animosity between you.

✓ Identify someone within your professional network who has strong relationship-building skills (like a mentor) and ask them to coach or advise you on how you can improve your own approach to developing relationships.

Having the Right Conversations

You have very little time to make a good first impression. We had seen in an earlier chapter on how to handle that first 30 seconds, the social ritual part- shaking hands and introducing yourself. Now you must build on that first impression- you have to make that person feel good about being with you, even for a brief encounter.

According to studies, 75% of us feel awkward and shy when we meet new people and find it difficult to start a conversation with a stranger. People are afraid of being rejected, or saying the wrong thing or just not fitting into the group.

Here are a few thoughts for ensuring the right conversations at any Events

- ✓ Reflect on why you are there. Consider the purpose/context of the dining experience. Is it part of a job interview process? A formal or informal gathering of co-workers? A business deal? A major project or sale? A partnership deal?

- ✓ Come prepared accordingly: Remember that business dining is all about conversation. So come prepared with appropriate dinner conversation. You need to contribute to your table talk in a way that sets other dinner guests at ease. So do all your research in advance. Who will be attending? What interests might they have? What topics are in line with the focus of the function? When the inevitable lapse in conversation occurs, know leading questions that will encourage table guests to begin talking about themselves.

Questions or statements such as: "I'm interested in knowing a little about the kind of work you do." "Please tell me about your interest in the organization represented here." "Have you heard the speaker before?"
- ✓ Be well informed
- What are the current events for today? Do you have small talk options ready for the function, if needed?
- Read at least one daily newspaper and a weekly news magazine
- Before going to an event, read the headlines of the day. Current events are perfect for small talk. And don't forget the sports and arts pages.
- Bring up these topics during the first conversational lull; the other person will be grateful for your filling the silence and will most likely follow your lead.
- ✓ Be Curious: It's not about you. Try focusing more on the other person.
- ✓ Wait for the host to initiate a discussion: Generally, the host initiates the business discussion. Business, if not urgent, is often discussed toward the end of the meal or over coffee. If you are the host, it's your job to steer the conversation, to suggest topics for discussion, and to make sure that everyone at the table is given the opportunity to be part of the general conversation. When the table isn't involved in a general discussion, be a good conversationalist with the people seated on either side of you.
- ✓ Pay attention to the thread of conversation and participate when appropriate. Don't

interrupt or repeatedly turn the topic of conversation to you or your interests.

✓ Take a glance at the person to see if there is anything about them that could start a conversation. People will be flattered by and appreciate your interest in them.

✓ If you're at a concert, trade meet- talk about the group, the room, food, entertainment. The same goes for wherever you may be.

✓ Try to choose universal topics of conversation in which all may have an interest. If you can't think of anything to say, then just listen attentively, and ask questions to generate conversation.

✓ Ask them appropriate, relevant questions about themselves-to start the conversation. Listen actively and show appreciation as they speak. Your conversation partner feels important when you ask questions; people like to talk about themselves, so let them do it.

✓ When you ask questions, there is a lot less pressure for your partner- you are perceived as caring, open and humble. Be a good listener! Ask OPEN ENDED questions that lead to longer answers. These types of questions usually ask who, what, when, where, why, and how, and use verbs that deal with your senses. (Covered separately under a different chapter)

What do you think of…?

How do you know so and so…?

What got you into…?

What gave you the idea…?

Describe….tell me about.

It's a good idea to prepare some questions before you go to an event. That way you'll have something to fall back on.
✓ Now share brief, reflective relevant comments about yourself if asked.
✓ Have only one conversation at a time
✓ Don't dominate the table. Give everyone a fair share to speak. And remember that you are responsible for conversing with your "triangle."

Conversing with your "Triangle"

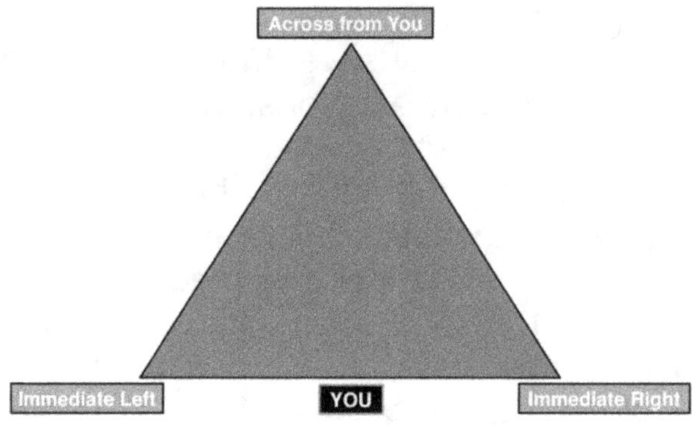

✓ Pay attention to people's physical needs. Do they need another drink? Something more on their plate?
✓ Avoid a loud tone of voice. Do not use profanities. Be sensitive to others before initiating conversation on topics that may not be suitable- avoid anything of a vulgar, graphic, or otherwise unpleasant nature. Ensure the conversation is entirely free of controversial subjects-Never tell jokes, as you never know who you could offend.

✓ If you are someone else's guest, even if part of a group, don't criticize the food, restaurant, etc. - this can cause embarrassment on the part of the "host."

Starting a conversation
A good place to start is to think of common interests. For starting a conversation or breaking the ice with strangers, think of: F.O.R.M.
F-Family
O-Occupation
R-Recreation
M-Money (economy)
Small talk can be a real saver in many situations. It fills the voids in conversations, helps ease tense moments, sets others at ease, and helps one become acquainted with others. There are two ways to make initiating small talk a little easier.
✓ The first is to be well-informed. To be able to discuss topics such as current best-selling books, news events, famous people, fitness crazes, technological advances, travel, and sports. These are all appropriate small talk subjects.
✓ The second way to ease into small talk is by asking others about themselves, their family, work, or hobby.
Here are some topics that are appropriate to speak up and get you started:
Small Talk Topics
✓ Your location or venue
✓ Shows, movies, plays, etc
✓ Art
✓ Food, restaurants, or cooking
✓ Their hobbies

- ✓ Their professional interests and responsibilities
- ✓ Sports
- ✓ The climate
- ✓ Travel
- ✓ Their local shopping favorites

Good Topics

- ✓ Current events, news etc
- ✓ Emerging Trends, Best Practices (Eg. How's business been amidst recession/ challenge etc?)
- ✓ Career Journeys + Performance/Burn Out Advice
- ✓ Food
- ✓ Memberships
- ✓ Mutual friends
- ✓ Hobbies
- ✓ Industry talk
- ✓ Styles/ Trends
- ✓ Sports

Bad Topics

- ✓ Any personal issues such as: family, health/ illnesses/ divorces/ separation/ affairs etc which may trigger something
- ✓ Religion/ religious beliefs
- ✓ Politics
- ✓ Salaries/ financial situation
- ✓ The cost of things
- ✓ Off color jokes- Racial, ethnic, and sexually oriented jokes
- ✓ Gossip
- ✓ Weight, height, shoe size, age or mental health

Here are some ways of opening a conversation for various situations:

For Prospects/ Customers:

- ✓ What were some of the key initiatives you took that brought you this far?
- ✓ What makes you stand out from your competitor?
- ✓ What's the most exciting thing about your business?
- ✓ What's the most exciting thing about your team?
- ✓ What are some of the most significant changes in your industry in recent years?
- ✓ If you could go back one year in time, what would you do differently?
- ✓ I'm honestly curious to know your story
- ✓ Tell me about your...?
- ✓ What's your company's biggest priority right now?
- ✓ How has business changed since we talked last?
- ✓ How are your efforts in [related business area]?
- ✓ What can I do to help you achieve....?

Common event

- ✓ What do you think of the conference so far? ... How have the sessions been? What did you particularly like?
- ✓ What inspired you to become a member of this body?

Company/Job

- ✓ Tom mentioned of how you were recently given additional responsibilities...Congratulations!

✓ How do you like this new role? What are some of the new areas responsibilities now? How different is it to what you were doing?

Business/Industry

✓ Off what I know, you were all along into production? How and what made you get into this active sales role?

✓ How have the recent changes in the government regulations affecting your business?

Location

✓ I live in Delhi. Where are you from?

✓ This is my very first visit to Mauritius. What do you recommend I see while I'm here?

✓ What is it that you like about living in Colombo?

Sports

✓ I hear that your favorite past time is playing golf. Did you see the xxxx Cup this year?

✓ Last night's cricket match kept me in real suspense. What did you feel about it?

Travel

✓ Sarah was mentioning that you just returned from Turkey. How was your trip?

✓ I know you'd been to Israel recently. Our family is also planning a trip sometime next year. How do you recommend we go about this?

Hobbies/Interests

✓ I noticed that you volunteered in the company's cancer prevention drive? That's certainly a good deed to do. How did the event go?

✓ What are your hobbies or interests outside of work?

Some Common Conversation Killers
How do you know if a question is too personal? Ask yourself how you would feel if someone asked you the question and everybody in the room could hear the answer. If you'd feel comfortable, the question is OK.
Avoid:
- ✓ Bragging
- ✓ Interrupting
- ✓ Monopolizing
- ✓ Not playing the game

If someone asks a question, give him or her something to work with. Don't do this: "How was your vacation?' "Fine"
Instead: "How was your vacation?" "Fine The beach was great and we went boating every day."

With your Boss
When you are out with your boss for lunch or dinner...
Here are a few points you can keep in mind while on a dinner/lunch with your boss.
- ✓ Focus on your attire-Dress Professionally
- ✓ Be punctual and on time
- ✓ Be active and enthusiastic all the time
- ✓ Watch your body language and mannerisms
- ✓ Maintain a presence of mind and positive attitude
- ✓ Let your host take the lead
- ✓ Stay focused
- ✓ Pick appropriate topics- do some groundwork, know what to talk about
- ✓ Matchup to the audience at food and drinks
- ✓ Express your gratitude

Things to talk while having lunch or dinner with your boss:
- ✓ Sports
- ✓ Music
- ✓ Literature: depending on his/her age
- ✓ Office history: their years of experience, his/her climb up, his/her challenges
- ✓ Assignments/ Projects
- ✓ Food
- ✓ Hobbies

Few things which your boss may want to hear from you
- ✓ Things you enjoy doing
- ✓ Things you find boring
- ✓ About your knowledge gaps
- ✓ Feedback and goals
- ✓ New innovative methods to implement
- ✓ How your life has been influenced by the company
- ✓ Career progression

Things to avoid talking while having lunch with your boss:
- ✓ Don't get too personal:
- ✓ Strictly avoid prejudiced topics
- ✓ Do not blabber/ blurt out others mistakes
- ✓ Be careful about your remarks: Think of the repercussions before you speak
- ✓ Do not whine or complain
- ✓ Never talk office politics/ gossip
- ✓ Toilet humor
- ✓ Indiscretions: You cross your limit and lose the impression in front of the boss

Effective Networking Skills

What is Networking?
The action of interacting with others to exchange information, ideas, and resources and develop contacts which can be for mutual benefit

Why Network?
75% - 80% of business is obtained as a direct result of some sort of networking.
There is some truth in the old saying: "It is not what you know, but who you know."
 Networking is the key to your business success

What are the main benefits of Networking?
- ✓ Access to knowledge through contacts
- ✓ Develop contacts that can provide with support and advice
- ✓ Learn from other people
- ✓ Create collaborations
- ✓ Can create otherwise unknown chances for collaboration and new opportunities.

- ✓ Development of your emotional and creative intelligence though added support and advice, including the support from mentors and champions
- ✓ Exposure to new environments
- ✓ Increase your confidence

The Key Steps to Networking Successfully

The best place to network is to begin in your comfort zone

Step 1: Your Comfort Zone: Your comfort zone will be in the areas you know, namely: what you want, who and where you are

- ✓ Your Agenda
- ✓ Your Story
- ✓ Your Questions
- ✓ Your Conversations
- ✓ Your Connection Points

Step 2: Your Objective: Before attempting to network-online or in-person, it's important to resolve in your mind the question of why. Why are doing this? What's your agenda? What is your objective of networking? What are the likely groups that you could get into? Who do you need to talk to? Target people/organizations? What do you want to achieve or find out? Where do you hope it will lead you?

How could you contact them?

- ✓ Looking up their profile
- ✓ Networking at events
- ✓ Asking connections

Step 3: Make a start by joining the Networking Groups you decided on in the earlier step. One recommended way to begin networking is to join at least two organizations. One networking group related to your target market and another of your peers. The target market group will allow you to meet people who you would like to work with and promote your business, whereas the peer group is for gathering knowledge in your field by hanging out with others like yourself.

Step 4: Do your Preparation (This step is very important)

Write down who you need to talk to, and why you want to talk to them.

Consider also, what do you want to find out? Or where would you like this to lead?

In other words, it's important to know your purpose - and in doing so you can increase your satisfaction levels afterwards.

You must have a compelling Story: Your Elevator Speech (See more on this in another earlier chapter) How do you present yourself in different contexts? And this can often be the most difficult part of any event – how to introduce yourself to strangers.

Your goal should be something like:

1. Introduce yourself to the people in your core group – these can simply be the people near you in a lecture or virtual breakout room. Try and find a connection point. Are you a trainer helping in skills they might find useful? Did you once work with one of their collaborators, mentors or trainees? Your aim should be that they remember meeting you.

2. Ensure that people in this core group know what specialty and industry you are in. Prepare your specific 'attention-grabbing' statements to answer the questions "Who are you and what do you do?"

Preparing a "story" (Elevator Speech or if you like a "statement of purpose") in advance will greatly help you settle in and take that first networking step.

Do your Homework on the Networking Group/ Event!

Things to do BEFORE the networking meeting or event:
1. Get a list of attendees
   - ✓ Ask the host or facilitator
   - ✓ Enquire online
2. Search for attendee's websites
   - ✓ Gather information
   - ✓ Review company services
   - ✓ Look at their picture
3. Select the people you want to meet
   - ✓ Write down their names
   - ✓ Call them before the event
   - ✓ Seek them out at the event
4. Ask the host or facilitator to introduce you to 2 or 3 people
   - ✓ People who would typically be a referral source
   - ✓ People who may be a potential client
   - ✓ People who are mover's and shaker's

Think about:
- ✓ What do you want to find more out about?
- ✓ How are you going to bring these questions into conversations?

Things to bring to the meeting or event:
- ✓ Have plenty of business cards with you (at least 50)
- ✓ Place business cards in your left pocket
- ✓ Name badges (if applicable)

Things to DO at the meeting or event:
- ✓ Get there early and stay late
- ✓ Introduce yourself within 60 seconds of entering the room

Step 5: What Impression do you want to create: Your first 30 Seconds Count!

"You only get one chance to make a <u>first</u> good impression."
First Impressions

- ✓ Dress for the Occasion: 60% of people are visual communicators. This means that to 60% of the world-image is key.
- ✓ Demeanor: Business entrance should be professional and quite seamless and understated.
- ✓ Introductions: Person of higher rank receives the introduction. Use the name of higher-ranking person first.
- ✓ Handshake and Share Business Card (See more on this in another chapter)

Step 6: Working your way around in the Event

1. Meet new contacts
- ✓ Do not hang with people you know
- ✓ Meet people you want to do business with
- ✓ It is not a card gathering experience
2. Look for groups of 2 or 3 people
- ✓ Get into groups already formed
- ✓ An easy way to introduce yourself to a group is "Do you mind if I join your conversation?"
- ✓ If approaching a speaker or any other group official have something relevant to ask e.g. 'I thought X part of your paper was really interesting, in particular I wanted to ask about...'
3. Seek information first
- ✓ Get others to reveal their wants and needs
- ✓ Let others shine and feel good about themselves
- ✓ Make others believe that you are listening and are interested

- ✓ Look at the other person for approximately 60% of the time. Give plenty of eye-contact but be careful not to make them feel uncomfortable.
- ✓ When listening, nod and make encouraging sounds and gestures.
- ✓ Use the other person's name early in the conversation. This is not only seen as polite but will also reinforce the name in your mind so you are less likely to forget it!
- ✓ Smile!
- ✓ Try to ask the other person open questions (the type of questions that require more than a yes or no answer).
- ✓ Avoid contentious topics of conversation.
- ✓ Use feedback to summarize, reflect and clarify back to the other person what you think they have said. This gives opportunity for any misunderstandings to be rectified quickly.
- ✓ Talk about things that refer back to what the other person has said. Find links between common experiences.

4. Give your "elevator speech"
- ✓ Reveal how you can help them
- ✓ Briefly explain what you do and how you do it
- ✓ Build their curiosity and interest in you

5. Conversation conclusions
- ✓ If you want to do business, conclude your conversation with offers and requests
- ✓ Send follow-up materials
- ✓ Introduce them to a colleague
- ✓ Ask for a business card
- Say something like *"It seems as though it would be worth following up with a more specific discussion. Would you be open to*

meeting up after the conference?" or *"I will call you tomorrow and see if we can help each other, okay?"* If they agree to a meeting see if you can schedule it right then and there with your smart phone and ask if they have theirs.

6. If you do not want to do business, conclude your conversation:

- Do not exchange business cards
- Use *the great escape* exit: *"I have enjoyed meeting you and I look forward to seeing you again."*
- Or to make a graceful exit. *"I have to make a quick call"*, or *"I'm going to get a drink of water if you'd excuse me?"* or *"I just spotted someone else I need to speak to, lovely to meet you."* or *"I've enjoyed meeting you. I know you have others you would like to meet and so would I . . ."*

Step 7: After the Event

Take time to write notes on the back of (their) business card or by using the Contacts App on your phone.

Review notes you have made

1. Write a quick note or send an email: remind them that you met them at the event and what you spoke about.
   - ✓ Send it soon after the event (within 24 hours)
   - ✓ Keep it simple and friendly
2. Send an article or useful resource
   - ✓ Relevant article, important telephone number or website
   - ✓ Make sure it is simple and helpful
3. Send a thank-you note for suggestions, ideas, and resources resulting from your contact. Show appreciation

4. Do them a favor
✓ Introduce them to associates, clients and vendors
✓ Help them to achieve their goals
5. Send them a referral. Ask for a follow-up call
6. Send a gift
✓ Make it appropriate
✓ Always add a note
7. Keep contacts on your mailing list
✓ Use contact management software for tracking
✓ Persistence pays

Name Placement Tags or Badges

Name badges are always worn on the right hand side of your front shoulder area. Why? The reason is that as you extend your hand in greeting, the gaze of the person you are meeting can easily follow your extended arm back allowing for a natural progression for the eyes to the name tag.

Some other good tips include:

✓ Arrive early. Arriving before the venue is noisy and full of people lets you get accustomed to the sights and sounds of the room before they become overwhelming. You can also scope out places to retreat to if you need a moment of solitude.
✓ Arrive with a friend or colleague. Not knowing anyone can be uncomfortable. Walking in with a friend guarantees you will know at least one person in the room who can introduce you to others.
✓ Have strategies to re-energize mid-event. Give yourself a networking time limit and then

go somewhere to regroup in solitude. Or consider taking a break to peruse the display items on the shelf or elsewhere. Sometimes you just need to be seen and not heard.

Rules for Business Introductions
- ✓ Know the status and rank
- ✓ Know the first and last names
- ✓ Pronounce each person's name correctly
- ✓ Know some piece of relative information
- ✓ Knowledge of person's job
- ✓ Use formal, academic or political title before last name
- ✓ Mr., Mrs., or Ms.
- ✓ Use formal introductions for senior-ranking executives
- ✓ Repeat person's name
- ✓ Name Tags do not replace proper introductions

And Finally…Some Deadly Networking Mistakes
- ✓ Hanging around your friends
- ✓ Staying too long in one group
- ✓ Being too busy eating and drinking
- ✓ Talking nonstop
- ✓ Asking about the weather or other irrelevant topics
- ✓ Getting pushy about meeting socially
- ✓ No follow-up or follow-through

Tips to Negotiate Effectively

What is Negotiation?
The authors of *'Getting to Yes'* define negotiating as a *"back-and-forth communication designed to reach an agreement when you and the other side have some interests that are shared and others that are opposed."*
A lot of people hate negotiations, not realizing that we negotiate every day, on a regular basis. Most of us face different types of negotiations throughout our personal and professional lives…
During an average day, we may negotiate with:
- ✓ The boss, regarding an unexpected work assignment;
- ✓ Subordinates, regarding unexpected overtime;
- ✓ A supplier, about a problem with raw materials etc;
- ✓ A banker, over the terms of a business loan;
- ✓ A government official, regarding the compliance with environmental regulations;
- ✓ A real estate agent, over the lease on a new warehouse;
- ✓ Your spouse, over who will walk the dog;
- ✓ Your child, over who will walk the dog (still an issue after losing the previous negotiation!)

Our ability to negotiate has been embedded since we were born. Remember, as a child when you wanted a particular toy and your mum or dad said *'No!'* What did you do next? You cried…you brought the roof down, till you got that toy!
So as we can see, negotiation is a common, everyday activity that most people use to influence others and to achieve personal objectives. In fact,

negotiation is not only common, but also essential to living an effective and satisfying life. We all need things- resources, information, cooperation, and support from others. Others have those needs as well, sometimes compatible with ours, sometimes not.

Negotiation is therefore a process by which we attempt to influence others to help us achieve our needs while at the same time taking their needs into account.

People often think about negotiation as just a method of getting their way. But it's really all about relationships.

The need for negotiation comes about because of a conflict of interests. What you want isn't what I want. But because we need to maintain a relationship, we decide to talk about our differences instead of walking away or beating each other up.

We search for a solution to our conflict of interests. We negotiate. And in the end, if the negotiation is successful, we get a solution we can both live with. It may not be perfect. You may not get all you want, and neither may I. But it's better than what we would have had if we hadn't negotiated and continued in conflict.

Exercise:

Here is a small challenge that I would like to start off with, to help you understand this subject more:
A father left 17 Camels as an Asset for his Three Sons. When the Father passed away, his sons opened up the will. The Will of the Father stated that:
-The Eldest son should get Half of 17 Camels (1/2),
-The Middle Son should be given 1/3rd of 17 Camels,

-The Youngest Son should be given 1/9th of the 17Camels

As it is not possible to divide 17 into half or 17 by 3 or 17 by 9, the sons started to fight with each other

Can you help them solve this!

(Go ahead…have a try before you see the solution below)

Solution:

They decided to go to a wise man. The wise man listened patiently about the Will. The wise man, after giving this thought, brought one camel of his own and added the same to 17. That increased the total to 18 camels.

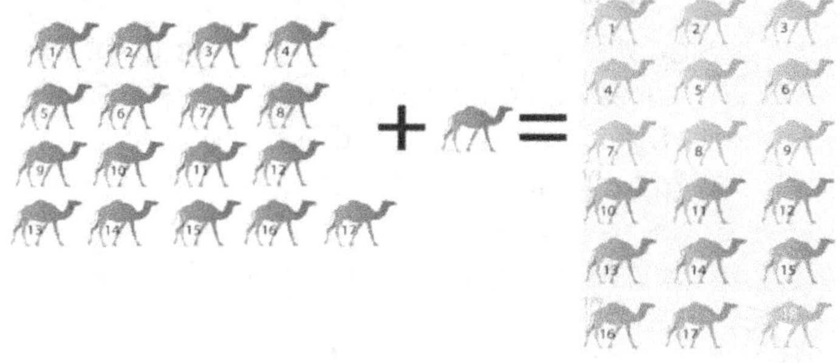

Now, he started reading the deceased father's will.

Half of 18　　= 9 *So he gave 9 camels to the eldest son*

1/3rd of 18　= 6 *So he gave 6 camels to the middle son*

1/9th of 18　= 2 *So he gave 2 camels to the youngest son*

Now add this up: 9 + 6 + 2 = 17

So this leaves 1 camel-which the wise man took back.

Here's the Lesson for you as a Negotiator!

The attitude of negotiation and problem solving is to **find the 18th camel- ie; <u>the common ground.</u>**

Once a person is able to find **the common ground**, the issue is resolved. It is difficult at times. However, to reach a solution, the first step is to believe that **there is a solution.**
If we think that there is no solution, we won't be able to reach any!

Negotiation Questions to ask yourself:
Preparation Checklist
1. What do I want from this negotiation? What are my Objectives: Outcome?
Must Achieve
Intend to
Like to
2. What options or alternatives would be acceptable to me? What are the other sides' objectives?
3. How does the other side see the negotiation?
4. What are my strengths—values, skills, and assets—in this negotiation?
5. What are my weaknesses and vulnerabilities in this negotiation?
6. Why is the other party negotiating with me?
   What is it that I have & they have?
   What is it that I have & they do not?
   What is it that I need more?
   What is it that the other side needs more?
7. What are the lists of Variables/ Concessions from your side?
8. What are the lists of Variables/ Concessions from the Customers' side?
9. How am I going to achieve my objectives in this negotiation?
10. What is the strategy of the other side likely to be?
11. What tactics should I use within the negotiation?
12. What tactics is the other side likely to use?

13. What lessons can I apply from past negotiations to improve my performance?
14. Where and when should the negotiation take place?
15. How long should talks last? What deadlines are we facing?
16. What are my interests in the upcoming negotiation? How do they rank in importance?
17. What is my *best alternative to a negotiated agreement*, or BATNA? That is, what option would I turn to if I'm not satisfied with the deal we negotiate or if we reach an impasse? How can I strengthen my BATNA?
18. What is my _reservation point_—my indifference point between a deal and no deal?
19. What is my *aspiration point* in the negotiation— the ambitious, but not outrageous, goal that I'd like to reach?
20. What are the other side's interests? How important might each issue be to them?
21. What do I think their reservation point and BATNA may be? How can I find out more? Who can help?
22. Who has more power to walk away?
23. Is there a *zone of possible agreement* (ZOPA) between my reservation point and the other side's? If there clearly is no room for bargaining, then there's no reason to negotiate—but don't give up until you're sure. You may be able to add more issues to the discussion.
24. What is my relationship history with the other party? How might our past relationship affect current talks?
25. Are there other differences that we should prepare for?

26. In what order should I approach various parties on the other side?

27. What is the hierarchy within the other side's team? What are the patterns of influence and potential tensions? How might these internal dynamics affect talks?

28. What potential ethical pitfalls should we keep in mind during the negotiation?

29. Who are my competitors for this deal? How do our relative advantages and disadvantages compare?

30. What objective benchmarks, criteria, and precedents will support my preferred position?

31. Who should be on my negotiating team? Who should be our spokesperson? What specific responsibilities should each team member have?

32. Do we need to involve any third parties (agents, lawyers, mediators, influencers, interpreters)?

33. What authority do I have (or does our team have) to make firm commitments?

34. Have I practiced/ role-played communicating my message to the other side? How are they likely to respond?

35. Does the agenda make room for simultaneous discussion of multiple issues?

What other questions would you add to this negotiation preparation checklist?

Negotiation Checklist:

Here's a systematic way to ensure you are well-prepared before your next negotiation

❑ ✓ Item accomplished

A. About You

❑ 1. What is your overall goal?

❑ 2. What are the issues?

❑3. How important is each issue to you?
Develop a scoring system for evaluating offers:
❑(a) List all of the issues of importance from step 2.
❑(b) Rank-order all of the issues.
❑(c) Assign points to all the issues (assign weighted values based on a total of 100 points).
❑(d) List the range of possible settlements for each issue. Your assessments of realistic, low, and high expectations should be grounded in industry norms and your best-case expectation.
❑ (e) Assign points to the possible outcomes that you identified for each issue.
❑(f) Double-check the accuracy of your scoring system.
❑ (g) Use the scoring system to evaluate any offer that is on the table.
❑4.What is your "best alternative to a negotiated agreement" (BATNA)?
❑5.What is your resistance point (i.e., the worst agreement you are   willing to accept before ending negotiations)? If your BATNA is vague, consider identifying the minimum terms you can possibly accept and beyond which you must recess to gather more information.
B. About the Other Side
❑1. How important is each issue to them (plus any new issues they have added)?
❑2. What is their best alternative to negotiated agreement (BATNA)?
❑3. What is their resistance point?
❑4. Based on questions B.1, B.2, and B.3, what is your target/ goal?
C. The Situation
❑1. What deadlines exist? Who is more impatient?

❑ 2. What fairness norms or reference points apply?

❑ 3. What topics or questions do you want to avoid? How will you   respond if they are asked anyway?

D. The Relationship between the Parties

❑ 1. Will negotiations be repetitive? If so, what are the future   consequences of each strategy, tactic, or action you are considering?

❑ 2. Can you trust the other party? What do you know about them?

❑ 3. Does the other party trust you?

❑ 4. What do you know of the other party's styles and tactics?

❑ 5. What are the limits to the other party's authority?

❑ 6. Check in advance with the other party about the agenda.

A Quick Glance at Negotiation

Set Objectives: Outcome
- ✓ Must Achieve
- ✓ Intend to
- ✓ Like to
- ✓ Options/ Alternatives acceptable
- ✓ Other sides Objectives

Information
- ✓ What is it that I have & they have?
- ✓ What is it that I have & they do not?
- ✓ What is it that I need more?
- ✓ What is it that the other side needs more?

Concessions/ Variables- Cost/ Value
- ✓ Price
- ✓ Delivery
- ✓ Schedule
- ✓ Place

- ✓ Training
- ✓ Payment
- ✓ Add-ons etc
- ✓ Trade concessions reluctantly
- ✓ Optimize yours
- ✓ Minimize theirs

Strategy

What is your Strategy? Have you role-played?

Tasks

If as a team, who will do what? When? At what stage?

Aim High

Keep whole package in mind

Silence! Sometimes it is best to **SHUT!**

During the closing stages you may need to find a negotiated solution that satisfies both parties.

As seen, Negotiating is not just about giving things away. It is about trading concessions to reach agreement. Most times a sales person will find that negotiating involves price issues.

The customer uses the price objection to gain a price reduction. If you have to give a reduction in price, always try to make it sound difficult and get something back in return

For Example: The customer says: "*Give me 10% discount and we have a deal*"

The temptation, as a salesperson is to agree and secure the sale. A good negotiator would react differently and try to win a concession.

"*This is extremely difficult, but if I am able to look at our discount structure, and if we were to go down that route I would then need a 2 year contract. Would that be possible?*"

If the customer agrees two year contract is possible, then we can offer 10%, or perhaps less

Your Interpersonal Skills when Overseas

Etiquette is heavily influenced by culture; each country and nation having their own set of rules for polite behavior. The world has more than 200 countries, with many containing multiple cultures. When dealing with an international clientele, or when conducting business in a foreign country, it's best to be aware of local etiquette guidelines. Knowing the proper business etiquette for the country of your potential client or partner is the key to success of your business transaction. By following respected and time honored business etiquette traditions, you will effectively demonstrate your own intellect and class, proving to your foreign business partners that you are worthy and deserving of their attention, respect and business.

Research and Preparation is Paramount: Preparation is the key to ensuring a positive impact: What may be good manners in one country or to one nation may not be good manners in another. Always take the time to research cross-cultural etiquette when dealing with a foreign client, or when conducting business in a foreign country. Awareness of international etiquette is important not just in face-to-face meetings but also in non face-to-face encounters such as sending gifts, conversing over the phone or communicating online. Areas you need to look at include: Religion, Dress code- what attire is appropriate, Social hierarchy, Use of titles and forms of address, Business card /Handshake exchange, Non-verbal communication -what is read between the lines, Introductions-how to get started on the right foot, Personal interactions- Topics to be discussed and not discussed, Valuing Time, Physical Space, Dealing with embarrassment, Gift exchange, How to work with an interpreter

General Tips

Here are some important points when dealing with other cultures:

- ✓ Some cultures dress conservatively as the norm. Americans tend to be more relaxed when it comes to dress codes, and even recommend dressing for comfort in certain fields and professions. People from other parts of the world are generally more conservative. The Japanese, for example, dress according to rank. Some Muslim nations find short dresses for women as offensive. If uncertain, stick to the safer side of conservatism.
- ✓ Some cultures meet and greet people with a kiss, a hug, or a bow instead of a handshake. A handshake for greeting is mostly universal. However, don't be surprised if you are occasionally met with a kiss, a hug, or a bow somewhere along the way.
- ✓ Stick to formal titles for business interactions unless invited otherwise. Approach first names with caution when dealing with people from other cultures. Some cultures are very hierarchical, and will consider it disrespect to be addressed without their title. Some cultures never accept first names in the business setting, and this should be respected.
- ✓ Some cultures are less time-conscious than others. Don't take it personally if someone

from a more relaxed culture keeps you waiting or spends more time than you normally would in meetings or over meals. Stick to the rules of punctuality, but be understanding when your contact from another country seems unconcerned.

✓ Understand differences in perception of personal space. Americans have a particular value for their own physical space and are uncomfortable when other people get in their realm. If the international visitor seems to want to be close, accept it. Backing away can send the wrong message

✓ Making eye contact: Don't be alarmed when a guest from France or Middle East locks eyes with you and gives a prolonged intense stare. This is common, in fact, the guest may move even closer to get better eye contact. The opposite is true with Britons. Each country will be slightly different in their non-verbal communication and the amount of personal space that they leave. Don't assume it is OK to touch someone.

✓ Business Cards: The degree of formality of business card etiquette varies from country to country. In general present your business card with both hands holding the top corners so recipient can read it. Also receive business cards with both hands when possible. It is considered respectful to spend time reading their card. Asians assume you will have a business card holder, so putting a card in your pocket is considered crude. Many nationalities like to have their language printed on the back to help translate the title (South America, Asia, and Northern Europe). Do not write on their business card, as this is defacing the card

✓ Body Language: Not only do other cultures speak a foreign language, the body language and gestures are different too. Showing the soles of your shoes while crossing your legs is very offensive with many other cultures. A finger on the nose means "confidentially" to a Briton. Nodding the head means "no" instead of "yes" in Greece and Turkey. Thumbs up is an offensive gesture in parts of Latin America and Africa

✓ Accepting a drink: Alcohol is common in many of the international cultures, so be prepared to be offered a drink. Do not turn down an offer of vodka from a business associate from Russia as this is considered highly offensive

✓ Gifts: Gifts are given to show gratitude, including as a way to thank someone for a hospitable act. If you are the host, it is not always appropriate to give a gift. Choosing the right gift and presentation is important - wrap the gift, using red or yellow paper - avoid white or black wrappers and ribbons

Give at the end of meeting, presenting and receiving with both hands but expect polite refusal at first. Other considerations: With Chinese, the gift must be given in a group setting or it will appear to be a bribe. With Japan, the gift should be wrapped or it may be considered rude- It's all about the box. Other cultures place meaning on symbols, colors and number. For example, a clock may be considered a death gift in China. The number 4 is extremely unlucky and will be taken with

offense in certain places. Do not open the gift unless you are invited to. Present your gift at the end of the meeting or agreed upon time. Be aware of the culture you are in when wrapping the gift. Always carry three levels of gifts to use as appropriate
- ✓ Topics to avoid: Jokes as some may not understand and they usually don't translate. Negative comments about guests' country's policies or policy makers, and religion, etc must be avoided

Here are some tips by specific country:
South East Asia
China
Being on time is vital
Use formal titles when introducing yourself. Have your business cards printed in Chinese and present business cards with both hands. Exchange business cards at the beginning of the meeting during the introductions. Include gold embossing on your card because it represents wealth, status, and prestige in Chinese cultures. Upon receiving your colleagues' business cards, read them attentively before putting them away carefully and respectfully. Putting a business card directly into your pocket without reading it is highly insulting to Chinese businesspeople. The way you treat the business cards indicates the degree to which you value your relationship with them.
Introduce and address your Chinese colleagues by title and last name, never by first name. During introductions, avoid overly strong handshakes because they are considered offensive and inappropriate for business meetings. Following the

introductions, start with small talk before moving on to more serious business matters.

Avoid direct eye contact. Do not offer gifts privately, as these are considered forms of bribery. Do not physically touch your Chinese colleagues.

Where possible, suggest "I'll look into," rather than the closed option of "No."

Wear conservative, dark, simple attire. Bright colors and/or ornate designs are considered flashy and inappropriate. Use conservative suits with subtle colors; Women should avoid high heels and revealing clothing

Do not only discuss business at meals. Speak slowly and pause between your sentences when speaking during a business meeting. At the table try every dish offered

The Chinese hosts should leave the meal first

Japan

Japan has the second largest economy in the world with about 130 million people that speak Japanese world-wide making it the ninth most common language- also the third largest group of internet users.

Avoid using harsh language, refrain from being confrontational and from openly disagreeing with your Japanese colleagues. The Japanese value trustworthy business partners.

Be prepared to answer direct questions such as "How much money do you make?" or "How old are you?" These questions are not considered offensive in Japan and are a way for your Japanese colleagues getting to know you

The customary greeting is a bow. It is proper to exchange business cards at the beginning of the meeting and be sure to take time to read your colleagues' cards before putting it away carefully and respectfully. It is customary to bow slightly when handing out your card. When toasting, do not lift your glass off the table. Respect personal space. Silence is valued in Japan, so do not force conversation at dinner. Do not be surprised if your Japanese colleagues go silent and close their eyes. This is a sign they are thinking critically.

Dress indicates status; dress to impress. Men should wear dark, conservative suits. Women should not wear pants and should wear low shoes. Do not slurp your noodles to indicate you have enjoyed them. It is appropriate for women to drink at dinner if the host orders drinks for the group

Korea

Present your business card with both hands, and, as with Chinese or Japanese associates, be sure to attentively read your Korean colleague's card before putting it away. Acknowledge those with highest status first, followed by the oldest.

Wear a dark-colored conservative business suit to meetings. When in a Korean business meeting, instead of directly saying "no", show your disagreement by inhaling through closed teeth, tipping back your head, and saying "maybe". When speaking to your Korean associates be sure to pause frequently to allow for questions and deliberations.

Send proposals and meeting agendas prior to the meeting to allow your Korean colleagues some time to review them. Expect your Korean colleagues to deliberate with each other before making a decision. Some of the values respected in Korea are: Certainty and structure, Collectivity and Team Work, Conformity, Loyalty, Obedience and respect for authority

Europe
UK
Attire should be conservative- Men should wear laced shoes preferably, formal.

Avoid personal questions or staring. Eye contact is rarely maintained throughout a conversation. Respect personal space. Business lunches are often conducted in a pub.

Do not discuss work at after-hours social events. Do not toast anyone older than you

France
Businessmen and women in French-speaking countries value formality and respect in a business relationship. Dress conservatively. Exchange of business cards is most often after initial introductions. Maintain eye contact during discussions. Exaggeration is interpreted as boasting, and even rude. Do not be afraid to debate with your French colleagues. Business partners who make logical arguments and have well rounded views are valued by the French. Avoid overly friendly behavior. Do not discuss business during meals.

Germany
German is one of the most widely spoken languages in Europe and two-thirds of all international trade fairs take place in Germany. Keep in mind that German business etiquette is strict and distinct from most other European countries.

Until you are personally invited to use a colleague's first name, address him or her by surname and title. Punctuality is paramount in a German business meeting so at all costs, avoid being late. Dress conservatively with minimal accessories. Maintain eye contact when speaking and listening. Shake hands before and after a business meeting with a firm, brief handshake to everyone in the room. Formally write up decisions and meeting notes and share them with your German colleagues.

Always knock before entering a room and allow those in higher positions to enter first. When a man and woman are of equal status, the man will enter first. Also, wait to sit until being instructed. The most senior-ranking individual will most often direct you.

Avoid extending meetings past their established schedules. Avoid exaggeration and high pressure talk.

Italy

When scheduling meetings, do it well in advance, with the most appropriate manner being in writing and reconfirming the same with a call. Business meetings are a time for each party to discuss ideas and issues, but not to make decisions, so avoid high-pressure tactics and do not expect decisions to be made. Expect your Italian colleagues to be descriptive, talkative and demonstrative. Italians value personal relationships, so third-party introductions are helpful.

Wear a few elegant accessories, as this display of wealth translates to power in the business arena. It is also very important to honor all agreed-upon verbal commitments in order to maintain credibility with your Italian business colleagues. In addition to a business card, it is important to have a social card, containing name, phone number, title, and academic degree, for non-business interactions.

Spain

Spanish businessmen will prefer to do business with people they know, so they may want to get to know you better through dinner or other social engagements before a business meeting takes place. Wear conservative business suits with a few accessories to indicate status and wealth, and to increase credibility. Communicate face-to-face whenever possible.

It is important to accept their invitations to prove your willingness to do business. Also, it is preferable that you be introduced to prospective Spanish clients through a mutual acquaintance. Once a business meeting is scheduled, do not be surprised if your Spanish associates arrive 15 minutes late. As always, you should arrive on time despite your colleagues' expected lateness. During meetings, expect Spanish colleagues to stray from the agenda.

Once a personal relationship is established, your Spanish colleagues will be loyal to you, not to the company you work for. Expect your Spanish colleagues to deliberate after a meeting rather than make a decision in your presence during the meeting.

Establish an oral agreement before drawing up a formal contract

Russia

Shake hands firmly and maintain eye contact while doing business with Russians. Wear dark, conservative business suits. Women should wear knee length skirts rather than pants-suit. Russians value patience and appreciate the opportunity to debate and digest negotiations. Avoid pressuring your Russian colleagues into making decisions, as this is considered rude and unprofessional.

While your Russian associates may not be on time for meetings, they expect that foreign counterparts will be punctual, if not early. Also, do not expect an apology from a tardy Russian colleague as they consider their behavior a test of your patience.

If discussing technical issues during your meeting, bring an expert along with you. Russians expect a thorough presentation and want to fully understand the topic before making a decision. Expect Russians to display emotion by becoming angry, storming out of meetings, or threatening to terminate your business in an attempt to gain the upper hand in negotiations.

Avoid showing the soles of shoes as this is considered highly disrespectful.

Middle East-Arabic Business Etiquette

Rather than greeting with a "hello" or "good morning," greet your Arab associate with the traditional Islamic greeting "Assalamo Alaikum," which translates to "May peace be upon you and may God's blessings be with you."

When planning a meeting, keep in mind Islamic principles and culture value structure. When choosing a restaurant, respect Islamic dietary restrictions. Some of your Islamic associates may not eat meat or pork so be sure there is an abundance of vegetarian options. Refrain from smoking cigarettes, drinking alcohol and consuming caffeine during meetings.

Certain values like consistency, loyalty, and respect for authority are very much respected in Arab countries. By creating and staying with a set agenda, you will demonstrate not only your organization and business savvy, but also your knowledge of and respect for Arabic business etiquette.

Bahrain: Smiling and direct eye contacts are essential parts of proper business etiquette in

Bahrain. Don't be surprised if your Bahrain partner gives and expects a kiss on the cheek upon greeting you!

Saudi Arabia: Outsiders are subject to Saudi Islamic law, which bans alcohol, drugs, pornography and pork.

United Arab Emirates: The lobbies of large hotels are the preferred venue for business meetings in the UAE, as these rooms limit distraction and give attendants easy access to refreshments.

Conclusion

In conclusion, let us remind ourselves that:
Life requires us to effectively manage 4 Key components if we have to be successful…
Think of the acronym **C.R.A.F.T:**
Change
Relationships
Attitude
Finances
Time
Anyone of these 5 components if not managed well, can lead to a disrupted life, and as we can see 'Relationships' is one of the essential keys.

Relationship building or Interpersonal skills are therefore crucial in business, helping create the foundation of care, trust and connection we need to grow. They enable us to get the best from teams and collaborators, and work towards your goals.

Whether you are working with someone who sits next to you or someone who works on the other side of the world, building relationships is most essential to achieving your objectives and those of the organization. A successful relationship is built on trust, respect and understanding, and requires ongoing investment from both parties. When difficulties arise in the relationship, they should be addressed openly and in a professional manner to ensure the relationship continues to develop

Inevitably differences of opinion will arise between leaders, managers, colleagues and external partners. But, good relationship building skills will help stop conflicts from escalating, and refocus on a better path. When problems do arise, these tools will see you through a crisis.

Building good work relationships can take hard work. It requires time, patience, and self-awareness. But putting in the emotional labor and building good work relationships will help you feel more connected to your colleagues and increase your overall job satisfaction. Healthy and positive work relationships will make your job less stressful and enjoyable. It will cut out the mundane factor that often plagues an employee in the long run. In fact businesses are increasingly looking for candidates with strong relationship skills. A company culture that encourages employees to maintain healthy relationships can go a long way towards enhancing employee well-being.

About the Author
'GERARD ASSEY'

Gerard Assey is a Graduate in Economics, a PGD in Management (HRD) and holds a Doctorate in Leadership. Gerard holds several International Qualifications in Sales, Debt Collection, Training & Teaching, and is a 'Fellow' of the prestigious 'Institute of Sales & Marketing Management'-UK, a Certified NLP Practitioner, a 'Certified Trainer', an 'Accredited Management Teacher-Behavioral Sciences', a 'Certified Competency Facilitator', a 'Certified Management Consultant'- (the International credentials of a professional management consultant, awarded in accordance with global standards of the ICMCI); and a Certification from the University of Michigan in 'Successful Negotiation: Essential Strategies and Skills'

He is also a Member of the 'National Association of Sales Professionals' backed with several years experience in varied industries, both in India and Overseas. He also holds an 'Etiquette Consultant' Certification from the USA (by Sue Fox, Author of Best Seller: 'Business Etiquette for Dummies'. She has trained some of the top celebrities' world over). He was also a recipient of a scholarship for extensive training in Japan on 'Corporate Management for India'.

Gerard Assey is 'Founder & Chief Corporate Trainer' of the Group: **'Citius, Altius, Fortius Unlimited'**- an organization that **celebrated 20 years of Glorious**

Service in 2021, focusing on 3 Core Competencies: **People. Performance. Profit**; in functional areas of Sales & Marketing, HR & Organizational Development, covering Recruitment, Training & Consultancy!

Having managed organizations with large Sales Forces in India & Overseas, his specialization cover extensive areas of Sales Training (All levels - Presentation, Negotiation, Key/ Strategic Accounts Management & Managerial Skills for all sectors), Bid Proposal/ Capture Planning/ Management Trainings, Retail Sales, Customer Service & Customer Retention Programs, Training for Prevention & Collection of Debt, Self & Personal Development Programs (Time Management, Teamwork & Team Building, Business Etiquette & Personal Grooming, Leadership & Managerial Skills, People Management Skills, Train-the-Trainer etc), including preparation of Custom-designed Business Manuals for Internal (HR, Induction, and Sales etc) & External use (Instruction, User Manuals).

Gerard has successfully conducted over 5900 Trainings & Workshops (as of Dec '22) all across India, Middle East, Africa, Europe & S.E. Asia. Besides public programs conducted regularly, both in India & Overseas, he has some of the top names as clients whom he services from Single Owners to large Public & Government undertakings, covering all sectors, for their in-house needs.

His website: www.CollectionSkills.com is the only one in this part of the world to be featured in the 'Collections & Credit Risk Magazine-USA' under 'Who's Who in Training' and ranks TOP, along with other websites listed below on most search engines.

Gerard is author of 51 books already (Dec 2022),
A few of the business related books being:

1. Bite-sized Bits on Commonsense Management
2. Heart to Heart on Life's Principles'
3. How to become a Successful Manager
4. The Sales Professionals' Master Workbook of S.Y.S.T.E.M.S
5. The Professional Business Email Etiquette Handbook & Guide
6. The Professional Business Video-Conferencing Etiquette Handbook & Guide
7. Professional Presentation Skills
8. Exceptional Customer Service
9. Professional Tele-Marketing Skills
10. Professional Debt Collection Skills
11. The G.R.E.A.T. Sales & Service Workbook
12. Sales Training Advantage for Results (*The Ultimate Sales Training Manual*
    to enable you stand out as a S.T.A.R.)
13. CEO Daily Planner & Organizer
14. The Sales Professionals' Master Daily Planner
15. The Professional Debt Collector's Master Daily Planner
16. My Daily Planner & Organizer
17. MY EMERGENCY INFORMATION RECORD (Family Emergency & Peace of Mind Planner)
18. The Ultimate Therapist & Counselors Planner and Organizer
19. Building an Ethical Workplace
20. Managing Relationships at Work
21. Managing Business Meetings Effectively
22. Effective Delegation Skills
23. Goal Setting for Success
24. B2B Selling by Email
25. Professional Business Etiquette & Grooming
26. Dining Etiquette & Table Manners
27. Effective Networking Skills
28. Grooming, Etiquette & Manners for Teens, Young Adults & Future Leaders
29. InterPersonal Skills

Besides regularly contributing to business & trade journals, including international ones such as the 'Creative Training Techniques' and the 'Sales News' of the U.S.A, He is also a member of several prestigious bodies & trade associations, having participated in many Conferences & Workshops in India & Overseas.

Prior to his last assignment of leading & managing a large MNC as head, Gerard had a 3-year stint in the Middle East as a Consultant with a leading British Consultancy Firm.

As the past 'Official Country Representative' for the International Business Award- 'THE STEVIES'-(the business world's own Oscar) for about 4 years- he ensured a few Indian companies that qualify for the same every year!

Gerard can be contacted at:

Email: training@Sales-Training.in,training@CollectionSkills.com
Websites:

      www.Sales-Training.in
      www.EtiquetteWorks.in
      www.CollectionSkills.com
      www.RetailSalesTraining.in
      www.SalesTrainingIndia.com
      www.ManualPreparation.com
      www.TrainingWithPuppets.com
      www.FirstContactAcademy.com
      www.SalesAndMarketingRecruiter.com

Our TRAININGS & BOOKS that can help your team

- ✓ **Sales Effectiveness**: Selling Skills for any Sector: Service/ Logistics/ FMCG Realty/ Insurance & Finance/ Media/ SPA's, Health Clubs & Salons/ Key Account Management, Effective Negotiation Skills/ Bid & Proposal Management Skills/ Retail Sales Training: Any Sector (Auto, Jewelry, Clothing, Luxury etc)
- ✓ **Customer Service Skills**-Complaints Handling & Customer Retention
- ✓ **Debt Prevention & Collection Skills**
- ✓ **Etiquette & Grooming**
- ✓ **Leadership & Managerial Skills**
- ✓ **Self & Personal Development Skills**: Presentation Skills/ Effective Communication Skills/Business Proposal Writing Skills/ Problem Solving & Decision Making Skills/ Empowering Secretaries-The perfect PA! (For Secretaries & PA's)/ Effective Time Management/ Teamwork & Teambuilding/ P.R.I.D.E- **P**ersonal **R**esponsibility **I**n **D**elivering **E**xcellence

A Few of Our Business Books
By the Top Corporate Trainer & Author of 50 Books! (Dec '22)
And...DAILY PLANNERS for Every Corporate Need!
Available Online on all leading Stores